Get to the Top of the Class:

How to Succeed in High School

To you, the reader,
and to my brother and best friend, Nicholas:
Education is life's key to success.
Use this book to fulfill your potential
and to enjoy your time in high school.

To my mother and father:
Thank you for your guidance, support,
and love, and for teaching me to value
what truly matters in this life.

Get to the Top of the Class:
How to Succeed in High School

Your personalized guide to academic success
(School & Library Edition)

by

Grace M. Charles

Valedictorian, Stern College for Women, Yeshiva University, NYC

Medical Student, Mount Sinai School of Medicine, NYC

GRACIE MANSION PUBLISHING CORPORATION

NEW YORK

Published by Gracie Mansion Publishing Corporation in association with CreateSpace.

Gracie Mansion Publishing Corporation
235 East 95th Street, Suite 17F
New York, NY 10128

To order books or for customer service call (646)929-4898.

ISBN-13: 978-1-4404486-3-8
ISBN-10: 1-4404-4863-9

Printed in the United States of America

Preface

In your hands you now hold the master key to a rewarding academic career and a successful, fulfilling life. More than ever before, young people want to succeed. But today's emphasis on a positive self image is, in and of itself, inadequate to ensure that success. With this book you will learn *how* to succeed, in much the same way that you learned how to add and subtract years ago when they taught you arithmetic. They do a great job teaching math in school, but they don't have a course on success in school.

After you learn the techniques here in this book in order to succeed in school, you will find that you value them as tools for success outside of the academic world as well. With the deliberate use of these strategies, you will determine your own future as opposed to letting others or circumstances determine it for you; that is the meaning of success. Right now, school is a very important part of your life. There is no reason not to start your success in life right away.

James G. Charles

EDITOR

> *Knowing is not enough, you must apply; willing is not enough, you must do.*
>
> *-Bruce Lee*

Contents

➢ Preface, v

➢ Introduction, xi

➢ 1. The Smart Attitude, 1
  o Self-reliance, 1
  o Your Main Goals, 3
  o Interest and Motivation, 5
  o The Focus, 8
  o Positive Confidence, 11
  o The Commitment, 12
  o Summary, 18

➢ 2. Life Preparations, 19
  o Family and Friends, 19
  o Networking, 23
  o Choosing Classes and Teachers, 25
  o Summary, 31

➢ 3. Organizing for Success, 33
  o Tools for School, 33
  o Tools for Home, 36
  o Time Management, 41
  o The Race to Bed, 44
  o Scheduling, 50
  o Summary, 58

➢ 4. In the Classroom, 59
  o Classroom Behavior, 59
    ▪ Your Peer Review, 60
    ▪ The Real Rehearsal, 61
    ▪ Talking with Your Teacher, 63
  o Taking Notes, 66
    ▪ What to Write, 66
    ▪ How to Write It, 68
      • General Note-taking Format, 69

- Comparing and Contrasting: T-Charts and Venn Diagrams, 72
- The Pyramid Method, 74
- The Cycle Diagram, 75
- The Tree Design, 76
  - When You Have a Question or Fall Behind, 77
  - Writing Quickly and Efficiently, 80
- Summary, 84

➢ 5. At Home, 85
- Reviewing Your Notes, 85
- Reading the Text, 90
  - Long-term Reading Assignments, 90
  - Increasing Your Reading Speed, 91
  - Improving Comprehension, 91
  - Improving Retention: Outlines, 93
  - Reading a Math Textbook, 97
  - Supplementary Readings, 98
- Doing Your Homework, 99
- Summary, 102

➢ 6. Test Time, 103
- Test Preparation, 103
  - When, 103
  - What to Expect, 105
  - What to Review, 108
  - Where and with Whom, 109
  - How, 111
    - Creating a Study Guide, 112
    - Over Twenty Techniques for Comprehension and Retention, 114
  - Your Final Hours, 125
- Taking the Test, 127
  - Testing Techniques, 128
  - Understanding the Question, 132
  - Answering the Question, 133
    - Responding to Free Response and Essay Questions, 135
    - Responding to Multiple Choice Questions, 137

- *Responding to Fill in the Blank Questions, 139*
- *Responding to Short Answer Questions, 140*
- *Responding to Matching Questions, 141*
  - *Spotting Tricks, 141*
  - *When You Don't Know, 144*
  - *Asking for Extras, 147*
    o *When You Get the Test Back, 148*
    o *Stress Reducers, 150*
    o *Summary, 154*

➤ *7. Doing Reports, 155*
  o *Choosing a Topic, 155*
  o *Researching, 157*
  o *Your Thesis, 159*
  o *Organization, 159*
  o *Writing Style, 160*
  o *Citing Sources, 163*
  o *Editing, 164*
  o *Oral Presentations, 166*
  o *Summary, 171*

➤ *Parting Message, 173*

➤ *Appendix: Sites for Students, 174*

➤ *My Notes, 175*

➤ *Author's Biography, 177*

Introduction

High school is a defining time in life, during which our success in school ever increasingly affects our lives and futures as adults. How well you do in high school directly impacts the colleges and programs to which you will be accepted, your knowledge and talents as a student, and your work ethic and overall character. You are building lifelong habits now.

When I saw some students not doing as well as I knew that they could do in school, I wanted to help them. I looked through countless academic help books, but soon realized that nothing on the market was both as thorough and as concise as such a guide must be. Succeeding in school is not simply a matter of picking up a few mnemonics (systems to improve one's memory) or learning a new way to take notes; there is much more to it than that. Succeeding in school requires maintaining a successful mindset, working efficiently while multi-tasking, balancing social life with academics, keeping oneself healthy and relaxed, and more.

> *Education is not a preparation for life; education is life itself.*
>
> *-John Dewey, influential educational reformer*

This guide is comprehensive. In it, I cover all aspects of what you need to know to succeed in high school, college, and beyond. The approach I describe here is the same one that I used throughout my later years of high school and during all four years of college—an approach that resulted in my being named valedictorian of my undergraduate institution.

This book will change your life, and you will enjoy reading it. Throughout it you will find noteworthy and interesting facts, quotes, stories, challenges, and more. Furthermore, I have integrated current research findings into the material, to enhance both the content of the book and the method in which the information is relayed to you. Students, educators, and parents will benefit. As an added feature, an appendix of useful online resources can be found in the rear of the book, where there is also room for your own notes, thoughts, and ideas.

> *You live what you've learned.*
>
> *-"Points of Authority" by Linkin Park*

Academic success is not the result of random chance or even of high IQ. Rather it is the consequence of the specific behaviors, actions, and strategies you will learn here. A good education will open many doors for you throughout life. Let's go get the keys!

All the best,

Grace M. Charles

1. The Smart Attitude

Your attitude says a lot about who you are. The ways in which you communicate with others, think of yourself, and manage your responsibilities are all consequent to your thought process. Therefore, to change anything about yourself, especially something as meaningful and significant as your academic life, will require a change in the way you think.

You are about to make some valuable adjustments to your daily routine and lifestyle. These changes will help you to improve your grades and to further your progress in school. You will exert yourself, overcome sizeable challenges, and maintain high academic standards.

Before we delve into the nitty-gritty of the process, it is important that you gain a solid foundation of confidence, motivation, and focus. These are the traits of successful students, and they define an attitude which we will call the *smart attitude*.

Self-reliance

It is the nature of academic work to be for the individual to master. Test questions are designed such that you must have an understanding of the material in order to answer the problems correctly. These questions require preparation and personal contemplation; no one else can do those tasks for you. Self-reliance is therefore a necessity for any student. The aim of self-reliance is for you to depend on yourself to put thought, time, and effort into the schoolwork you do. With self-reliance, you accept the responsibility of working hard to do well in school.

If you don't know the answer, *you* need to figure it out; if there is a gap in your understanding of a topic, *you* must fill it in. There will not always be someone else for you to ask or someone else to explain the answer to you. Under academic testing conditions, of course, there is no room for the sharing of answers.

The concept reaches even farther than the classroom. Let's look at a real-life example.

Say you are lost in the middle of New York City, and in your hands you hold only two things: a crisp $1 bill and a brand new map of the city. You need to get to Grand Central station to meet your friend, and you don't have much time. At first, you know what to do. With calm and confidence, you approach the nearest hot dog vendor, take out your $1 bill, and buy a large, toasty warm soft New York pretzel. As you chomp on the pretzel, all is going well, until you recognize the more difficult challenge still facing you: how will you get to the train station? You could always ask other people, but at any time, many of the people around you on the streets are out-of-towners themselves, or they do not speak English. Furthermore, you can't count on someone else being able to ensure that you get where you want to go. And, finally, didn't your mother tell you not to talk to strangers? With this established, the solution to your dilemma is frighteningly clear: you must figure out the route *yourself*. With flawless ingenuity, you unroll

 your nice new map and get those brain cogs turning. Even though you have rarely used a map in the past, you are able to get it all figured out: you identify the nearest intersection, locate your destination and the relevant streets on the map, and plot a course. The next thing you know, you are standing on the correct train station platform with your friend. As you chat, you feel great. You have just successfully navigated the streets of the world's greatest city, and your friend is enviously watching you enjoy a gigantic soft pretzel. Self-reliance enabled you to persevere and to successfully complete your mission.

While the example is simple, its message is far-reaching: When you stay in charge, you can ensure your own success. There won't always be other people around to help you, and there certainly won't always be *reliable* people around. This principle applies both in the academic setting and in the real world. Sometimes, your choice will be obvious, such as buying the pretzel, but at other times you will be pressed to think harder and to figure out more difficult problems, such as how to get to the train station.

Being self-reliant will allow you to accomplish great things, such as thinking with more creativity, communicating more effectively, and earning higher test scores.

Thoughts of Ralph Waldo Emerson, from his essay "Self Reliance":

I read the other day some verses written by an eminent painter which were original and not conventional. The soul always hears an admonition in such lines, let the subject be what it may. The sentiment they instil [Emerson's spelling of instill] is of more value than any thought they may contain. To believe your own thought, to believe that what is true for you in your private heart is true for all men, — that is genius. Speak your latent conviction, and it shall be the universal sense; for the inmost in due time becomes the outmost,— and our first thought is rendered back to us by the trumpets of the Last Judgment. Familiar as the voice of the mind is to each, the highest merit we ascribe to Moses, Plato, and Milton is, that they set at naught books and traditions, and spoke not what men but what they thought. A man should learn to detect and watch that gleam of light which flashes across his mind from within, more than the lustre of the firmament of bards and sages. Yet he dismisses without notice his thought, because it is his.

Your Main Goals

In order to become more successful in school, you need to decide upon and set goals. Worthwhile goals include high grades, matriculation into higher learning programs, more efficient and effective study techniques, positive relationships with teachers and classmates, or some combination thereof. As you read through this section, think over what your goals are; you will be recording them soon.

By being aware of the specific accomplishments you wish to achieve, you will be able to apply the soon-to-come techniques, strategies, and organizational methods directly to your aims as you proceed through this book. Furthermore, studies have found that those individuals who write down their goals are far more likely to achieve them than those who do not do so. Just like a contract, a written goal gives you a feeling of commitment and responsibility, helping you to succeed.

First, decide what your overall goal is. You may be aiming to gain acceptance into a competitive college or honors program, or looking to improve your GPA and class ranking.

In general, when setting goals you want to choose items that are both reasonable and challenging. Furthermore, your goals should include the 3 W's:

I'd like to introduce you to Nick. He's a sophomore in high school, and he has been maintaining a B average. Nick wants to elevate himself to a higher level of academic standing. Nick has committed himself to being self-reliant, and he will be our model success-seeking student.

Nick

addressing <u>wh</u>at you <u>wi</u>ll do and by <u>wh</u>en you will have it done. WHAT defines your objective; WHEN sets a deadline; the word WILL keeps you determined. You <u>will</u> achieve your goals!

Following this format, our model success-building student Nick wrote his two goals below.

Nick's Goals:

<u>I will raise my GPA to at least 90 (A-) by the end of this school year.</u>
<u>I will get accepted to the Honors Society by the January deadline.</u>

I will now ask you to decide on your goals and commit them to paper as well. It is best to get this done as soon as possible so that you will have something definitive on which to focus. Whether your goals aim higher or lower than Nick's, or even if they address entirely different topics, choose the goals that are right for you. Take time to carefully think about them so that you are sure to write down that which you truly want to achieve. Following the format of Nick's example above, write in the space provided what you want to and will accomplish. If you are still undecided, you can continue on and come back to this section when you are ready. *Remember to format your goals using the 3 W's.*

My Goals:

_____

_____

_____

_____

_____

_____

The aims you just specified will help you to direct your academic work. Furthermore, keeping these commitments in mind provides you with interest and motivation for your studies.

Interest and Motivation

You go to school in order to learn the information and the habits that are necessary to further yourself in society. Every day you take in and process new knowledge and insights, some of which can be quite interesting. This interest is valuable: you can use it to motivate yourself, to make the material more fun to learn, and to help you to remember the material for tests. When such an interest is not so easily forthcoming, you can still find ways to involve yourself with the material in order to reap these same benefits.

In high school, you often have to take classes because you are required to rather than merely because you want to. As a result, you will understandably at times find yourself uninterested in some of the material in certain courses. It is your duty in such situations to develop an interest. How? Try the following:

1) *Identify connections to your personal interests.* For example, if you are interested in keeping healthy, biology class might be of use. Learning about the human body's functioning and organization can help you to think of ways to take better care of your own body.

2) *Apply what you learn to your everyday life.* Course material can be of use in your nonacademic time. Consider, for instance, World Geography, a class which students often find rather dry. Global news, movies, magazine articles, and even casual conversations often make reference to locations with which many people are unfamiliar. This class will familiarize you with both the well-known and lesser-known countries of the world, enabling you to understand such references. Also, what you gain from this class will be useful to you in ways you do not yet realize, such as in making future financial investments, understanding world events, and voting for political leaders.

3) *Develop new interests from what you learn in the classroom.* Continuing with the World Geography example, such a course may spark your interest in finding out more about some of these previously unknown countries. For instance, while most people consider oil to come from the Middle East, did you know that the South

American country Venezuela produces more oil than Iraq (2.667 million barrels per day as opposed to Iraq's 2.094 million barrels per day [2007])? This could easily initiate debate on global policy. Or were you aware of the fact that the United States purchases more oil, natural gas, uranium and electricity from Canada than from any other country [2008]? Learning about other countries gives you a springboard from which you can jump into so many other topics of possible interest. Search them out and enjoy the results.

By making what you learn in class of interest to yourself, you will be able to better remember and apply the information later on. Taking a personal interest will also enhance your ability to have a positive attitude towards your schoolwork. Just as we were able to find reasons to take interest in World Geography, let's take a look at any boring classes you may have and find what makes them interesting.

Ask yourself the following questions.

- Why am I in this class in the first place?

- Is the information I learn here applicable in any way to my daily life?

- Will this information help me to better understand more advanced issues on the same topic?

- Can I use this knowledge in my daily conversations?

- Is this something about which my family and friends might be interested in hearing?

- Will what I learn in the class help me to do better in my other classes?

- Does this class teach me about something I would like to further to study on my own?

- _____

- _____

- _____

- _____

Use these questions to guide you in finding anything that may make an uninteresting class relevant to you. Try to think of broad questions tailored specifically to your interests, and fill them in on the lines above. For example, if you plan to have a career in nursing, you may ask if the class in some way will help you to better understand medical treatments and personal interactions in the health field. Apply this method to the necessary classes in order to find reasons to take genuine interest in them.

Invest yourself in what you are learning. Take an interest in the material. It will make you a more interesting person; and you will be able to use to your advantage the knowledge that you gain.

There are also other strategies you may employ to maximize your interest in your coursework. For many students, it helps to see academics presented in a different setting. For example, schoolwork can be analogous to athletics. In sports you must build up your strength and skills just as you must build up your knowledge and creative thinking abilities in academics. The days preceding the big game require careful preparation, as do those days before a test. Proper preparation and exertion will lead to victory over your opponents at the game, and the right academic preparation and thought will lead to an A on your next big exam. Need motivation? With athletics, your coach screams, your teammates cheer, and you want to win. Schoolwork is not that different. You want to succeed; you can cheer yourself on, make yourself keep going when the going gets tough, and come out on top in the end. Use your desire to do well to keep yourself going strong in school.

Finally, recognize that any topic can be interesting and a source of useful knowledge for some reason or another. Even if you cannot imagine such a reason, challenge yourself to think about the subject at hand *as if* it were fascinating. You may very well trick your mind into believing it.

Put effort into keeping yourself motivated and interested in your courses. Others may want to act as if everything the teacher says is boring. Let them; do not argue, but do not let yourself get sucked into their way of thinking. Everyone has their own preferences, and everyone has their own goals in life. You want to meet yours. If someone tries to get you to dislike or avoid going to a class, do not let that individual influence you. Someone else may find the

> *Happiness can be defined as doing what you are supposed to be doing.*
>
> *-Ancient Jewish Teaching*

A "ROLL" MODEL

When world-class basketball star LeBron James needed to improve his shooting, he knew what he had to do: focus. He stayed in the gym for two and a half hours every day working on his shot. More than that, he made his time meaningful, as he says, "I just tried to go hard for those minutes, and tried to make every shot count." LeBron knows that to really improve at something, it takes both time and maximum effort. When you want to succeed, the rest of your life takes a backseat to your work. And, LeBron says, his efforts paid off, "...this year I feel like, if people are going to give me the jumper [shot] I know it's going to go in." LeBron improved his game and his confidence because he focused every day on achieving his end result. This method will help you to reach your goal, just like it helped LeBron James to achieve his.

material daunting and difficult, but that person is not you. Set aside any negative thoughts others may have given you, and experience the class for yourself. Negative thoughts don't help you, and they will damage what could otherwise be an enlightening and interesting learning experience. Concentrate on keeping yourself interested in your classes and motivated to do well. In this way, you will be able to more easily focus on, learn from, and enjoy your courses.

The Focus

A good photographer knows: before taking any quality shot of an object, he must always focus his camera. Other objects in the picture often must be compromised so that the object of interest in the shot comes out correctly. Such is also true with your education. In order to succeed in school, you must put your focus on it. Other commitments need to take a backseat in order for you to achieve your objective.

What does this mean for your everyday life? Let's apply the idea of focusing to a common example. Say your friends want to go out to a movie with you tonight. You want to go, but you still haven't studied for tomorrow's science test. Although it most likely sounds much more appealing to go with your friends and skip out on a few hours of studying, you have trained yourself otherwise. As a focused student, your main objective for this day, like all other days, is to complete your academic commitments, which include studying for that science test. The point of this example is to show you that focus is not something you can broach passively. Rather, you must actively look to focus on your schoolwork and academic responsibilities and to vigorously avoid the many pitfalls and distractions along the way.

When it comes to focusing, half the battle is being able to recognize when you are being distracted. Only once you identify the destructive activity can you escape from it. One of the very worst offending items is what we call *the box*. The box is really a generic term for all electronic activities that are a waste of time, such as watching television, chatting online using instant messaging, going on Facebook or YouTube, playing video games, or zoning out to an MP3 player. These activities are addictive, take up lots of time, have negligible benefits, and are often difficult for you to pull yourself away from. In short, they are a huge waste of your time! To keep focused, you want to limit your time on the box.

In order to help you identify and eliminate distractions, try the following technique. Think about the activity in question and ask yourself, *Will this really have any positive impact on my future?* Consider the opportunity cost, i.e. what you will miss out on by partaking in this activity. In the example we used above, the opportunity cost of going to the movies with your friends would be the time you could have used studying, and therefore the higher grade you would have received on your test the following day. By using this method to weigh the pros and cons of an activity, you can accurately judge when you will be able to participate in a nonacademic activity without sacrificing much in the way of your schoolwork.

As we discussed before, getting your thoughts down onto paper gives you something concrete on which to concentrate, and a huge part of focusing on your schoolwork is concentrating on actively avoiding distractions. Therefore, it is a good idea for you to write down those activities that distract you in specific. Nick jotted down his distracting bad habits below.

Nick's Bad Habits

- *Going on Facebook*
- *Text-messaging on my cell*
- *Checking e-mail frequently*
- *Taking a lot of snack breaks*
- *Randomly surfing the internet*
- *Playing games on my graphing calculator*
- *Watching television*

As you may have noticed while reading Nick's list, most of his bad habits are not bad in and of themselves. Rather, they are bad in the context of not allowing him to stay focused on his schoolwork. Defining these time-hogging habits will help you to keep tabs on them so that they do not detract from your academic success. Take a moment to brainstorm and to write down all the activities in which you participate that waste your precious time. Think of as many items as you can so that you do not miss anything.

My Bad Habits

_____

_____

_____

_____

_____

_____

_____

_____

_____

_____

_____

_____

_____

_____

In order to be a successful student, you will no longer be able to participate in these activities to the extent that you have been. You need not entirely eliminate them from your life, however. In **Scheduling,** we will go over how you will be able to include these activities in your life while still accomplishing all of your necessary schoolwork.

While your peers may spend much of their time succumbing to the box and to other bad habits, you want to spend your time productively, taking the steps necessary to succeed in school. Distractions can come in many forms: family, friends, other students, the box, napping, snacking, etc. While certainly everyone needs a certain amount of rest and relaxation, do not allow this to become an excuse for you to waste time. You can improve both your focus and your free time by vigilantly keeping an eye out for and avoiding distractions.

Positive Confidence

Positive confidence is the final ingredient of the smart attitude and is a necessary part of being a self-reliant individual. Students who get high grades approach their work with the premise that they will be able to complete the work. Less successful students do not approach their work with such a confident attitude, and as a result they are more likely to give up when the going gets tough. After all, how can you depend on yourself to do well if you don't truly believe you are capable of accomplishing the item in question? It is time you acquire the attribute of positive confidence.

Simply put, positive confidence is self-confidence you create by giving yourself positive affirmations. For instance, when you are posed with a tough homework question, think a positive thought, such as *"I can do this. I have prepared myself well, and I have handled tough questions before. Now I will do it again."* Attack the problem with the knowledge that you will be victorious. Do not tell yourself *"This problem is too hard for me. I'm not smart enough. I can't do it."* Do not believe for one moment that you can't do it; surrendering to this negativity will not get you anywhere. As a self-reliant student, you know that when faced with a tough question, you can solve the problem on your own, and you will.

To drive the point home, let us consider a probable scenario including Nick and his not-so-successful classmate Clyde. For homework, their teacher assigns a difficult written assignment due the following day. When Clyde gets home, he takes out the assignment and immediately feels a knot form in his stomach. He thinks the questions look too hard. As he reads through each question, he becomes more and more convinced that he is incapable of answering any of the questions. Upset by the unfair assignment, a frustrated Clyde hastily fills in some answers, even though he knows they are probably incorrect. He figures that this way he at least has something written, and he hopes that he can copy a peer before class. Clyde decides he also will complain to the teacher about the difficulty of the assignment and possibly earn some pity points that way.

This is not at all the approach of success-seeking student Nick. Nick is focused on achieving his goals and is careful to approach the assigned questions with positive confidence. Even though he can tell the assignment is not easy, he is confident in his ability to answer the questions and remains cool, calm, and collected. He looks at the first question, and then, using the method and skills we will soon discuss, breaks the question into manageable pieces he can answer on his own. With time and thought, Nick methodically answers each of the assigned questions. He doesn't need to alienate his friends and teacher, hope for pity, or hold a grudge against his teacher for the "unfair" assignment. Most importantly, Nick ends up better understanding the information he needs to know for class and scoring well on the assignment.

As you can see, this scenario exemplifies the major role of positive confidence in producing quality schoolwork. Positive confidence can be the deciding factor between a well-done assignment and an incomplete one. You are committed to doing what it takes to succeed, and you are now learning exactly how to channel this willpower into action in

> *Where there's a will, there's a way!*

order to meet your goals. You and no other person are in control of the way you see yourself and of your attitude towards your schoolwork. Don't allow seemingly tough questions to derail your confidence. Have a positive self-image and put your trust in your abilities to succeed. Doing so will help you to maintain interest in your schoolwork, to be persistent when posed with challenges, and to stay focused on achieving your goals. Remember that your positive self-confidence is not self-deception; rather, it is self awareness. It is based on the commitments and competencies that you are truly developing now.

The Commitment

Now that you recognize the benefits a smart attitude has to offer you, you must be wondering how you can effectively develop this valuable trait in yourself. The answer is to commit to following independently each of the five steps listed on the next page.

The Five Steps

1) Define the problem at hand in terminology you can understand, and determine what kind of response the problem requires. Know what is expected of you to earn the highest grade.

2) Gather the required information and materials and perform any necessary reading and research. For a lengthy assignment, this can include searching databases and visiting the library. When you read the material, take notes and include source page numbers for your own reference and for making any necessary citations.

3) Apply what you know in order to take a position on the issue. In the humanities, this may be your thesis. In the hard sciences, this may be your hypothesis. For simple problem solving, this step asks you to determine which method or equation(s) will most efficiently provide the correct answer.

4) Write your well-organized response or essay, or answer the question. Perform any necessary calculations.

5) Check and edit your work.

Like a treasure hunt, completing one step in this process often will reveal what needs to be done in the succeeding step.

As an example, let us consider using the five steps in answering a free response question assigned for history homework:

```
Compare  and  contrast  how  World  War  I  and  its  outcomes
affected East Asia versus how it affected South Asia in the
period from the war through the 1930s.
```

While a question such as this can often seem like a whopper, it is in fact entirely doable for the self-reliant student, providing the five steps are followed. Let's walk through it.

In Step 1, you must understand what is being asked of you. You know that *to compare and contrast* means 'to examine and note the similarities and differences between the two regions. But you must also evaluate these differences in order to establish their significance. You need to know what to include in your response in terms of content; if there is an applicable grading rubric, refer to it. Your teacher may expect you to bring up specific historical facts and figures discussed in class, to draw relevant maps and diagrams, or to present any of a number of other items. Additionally, you will need to consider the format of your paper. Your teacher may expect the essay to be typed in a specific format, to be handwritten, to include a bibliography, or to have in-text citations. Once you are aware of exactly what you are responsible to produce, you are ready to move on.

Your second step is to gather the materials you need and to read and evaluate the information necessary to formulate your response. You may only need your textbook and class notes, or you may have to pick up further materials at the library. In the sample problem given, for instance, you would need materials to help you analyze the historical and geographical references, such as which countries were included in East and South Asia, when World War I took place, and what the war's outcomes were. Defining these variables will help you to identify the correct articles and books, especially if your class notes are not sufficient. First read your class notes and then read and take notes from any additional sources, selecting information that is relevant to the prompt. As you analyze what you read you move into the next step.

In Step 3, you use your own insights to establish something meaningful from what you are learning. Here you would learn that in WWI, the Indians of the South Asian Indian Peninsula fought for their colonizers, the British; and the Japanese attempted to consolidate their position in China through military action and threats while the European powers were busy elsewhere. From this information, you might determine that *colonialism fueled the war and helped to account for differences in the war's effect on East and South Asia*; this statement could even be your thesis. You might also consider that the Indians' disappointment that the Brits did not grant them independence for helping them during the war later led to the various peaceful and violent liberation movements in India. You could save this idea for your conclusion. Step 3 is important because only when you think about what you are learning and take some kind of position do you truly understand and own the knowledge.

In Step 4, you write your response, which must be laid out in a logical format, and answer the specific question being asked. This step is very simple when answering a short and straightforward question. In the case of a more lengthy report such as for the given writing prompt, you need to use your notes, texts, and thoughtfulness to create a coherent and well organized response.

For Step 5, you need to check over your work. In the case of a free response assignment, you would look over your work to correct any mistakes in syntax or grammar. On a multiple choice test, you would make sure you filled in the correct bubble to match your intended answer choice for each problem. In the case of a math or science problem, you would go over your calculations or, time permitting, confirm that you derive the same answer using a different method.

Devising your own responses to a question takes time, thought, and resourcefulness. Sticking to the five-step process will help you to create your responses in a systematic fashion, enabling you to be more efficient with your time and to produce a higher quality product. Looking at another student's answers may seem like an easy way to cut down on the amount of work you have to do, but doing so will rob you of your self-reliance and of an excellent opportunity for intellectual growth, and it is necessary that you experience that intellectual growth and obtain that knowledge in order to do well with exams, class

Your ABC's and 1, 2, 3's

Copying other students is harmful to your academic success. It may seem like a good thing because it requires so little of your time and thought. However, when you don't put thought into what you do, you don't learn from it.

Imagine if as a young child you had not made the effort to learn how to read, write, or count. If you had never thought about your school lessons, you would have never learned these vital skills. Fortunately, at that young age, you were probably eager to learn and to prove your independence as a thinker.

Rekindle in yourself this eagerness to learn. You are in school to learn, so make the most of it. Even when copying someone else may seem like the easy way in the short run, in the long run it is always a bad idea. You must learn and think for yourself in order to succeed. Develop in yourself an enthusiasm for independent learning and thinking, and you are on your way to becoming a truly educated individual.

discussions, and future assignments. Furthermore, it is unlikely that someone else's answers will be of the quality and caliber of answers you produce on your own. You must carry out each of the five steps on your *own*. Just like exercise, when the work gets the toughest is also when it will give you the greatest results. By taking the time to sit and think, consider your class notes and additional readings, and organize your ideas, you will be able to answer the questions and to complete your assignments entirely on your own.

When you think of your work in steps, it becomes more manageable. That is why a big part of the smart attitude is recognizing that almost all assignments can be completed by following the five steps. Successful students don't make the common mistake of seeing a large or tough assignment as one massive problem; rather they break it into doable pieces and steps, allowing them to complete the assignment without undue frustration. When the going gets tough for any assignment, apply the five steps. Doing so will enable you to maintain your self-reliance and to put out stellar results all while maintaining your cool.

The information you learn in this book will change your life for the better. I want that for you, and you want it for yourself. In order to meet that expectation, it is imperative you commit to following these five steps. Make a promise to yourself and to me right here and now that you will complete your assignments by following the five steps. It's worth your knowing that you really mean it.

I, _____, *endeavor to be self-*
PRINT NAME HERE
reliant as best I can. I will follow the five steps whenever possible and will not ask others to do the thinking for me. I am responsible for my success.

_____
SIGN AND DATE

The commitment you just made will enable you to enhance your intellectual abilities and will strengthen your confidence in your own capabilities.

By acknowledging that you are the one responsible for answering your own questions, you open yourself up to gaining the necessary rigor you need to be a successful student. While it may be easier to skip out on thinking for the moment, in the end it is the students who apply thought to their schoolwork who end up with the greatest understanding. If a problem is difficult, keep at it. If you don't know the answer, look in the textbook for more information. Self-reliance is a powerful mentality shared unanimously around the globe by successful students. As you progress through this book and gain the skills you need to succeed, your own efforts and dedication will transform you into a high-achieving and successful student. Welcome to the world of challenges, thought, knowledge, and reward!

Hello!

*We just went through a process you will see often throughout this book: **taking a problem and breaking it down into smaller pieces**. This is a common habit of successful students. A large complex question broken down into small and simple pieces allows you to better understand what is being asked of you and to more easily come up with the required information. This way, almost no problem will be too big for you to handle on your own.*

Whenever you see this little construction man drilling away, recognize that he represents breaking a large task into smaller, more doable pieces. This will allow you to recognize when you are employing this valuable skill.

SUMMARY: THE SMART ATTITUDE

- The benefits of self-reliance will help you to succeed both in school and in life.

- Write down your academic goals in the *3 Ws* format.

- Actively work to develop interests in your classes and motivate yourself to do well.

- Identify and eliminate distracting activities by considering opportunity costs.

- Record your particular bad habits and focus on avoiding them.

- Develop positive confidence in order to stay persistent in the face of challenges and to keep your focus on achieving your goals.

- Every assignment can be broken down into completing the five steps. Commit to following the five steps in order to simplify your work and maintain your self-reliance.

2. Life Preparations

It is often said that an ounce of prevention equals a pound of cure. The point of this bit of wisdom is that a small degree of preparation can save you from an exponentially larger quantity of work in the future. Applied to your schoolwork, this means that if you take certain small and simple steps now, you can better ensure your success later.

The people around you have an effect on you. Among other things, they can affect your mood, availability, attitude, and desire to work efficiently. Many students unwisely believe that their social environments are purely left to chance. However, this view is untrue and can be harmful. Your social environment is what you make it through your own choices and decisions. You can purposefully create a social environment conducive to your academic success and void of distractions and detractors. In this section we will discuss what such an environment entails and how to go about creating these surroundings. By forming a social life considerate of your academic goals, you build a solid foundation for your immediate success and for the ultimate achievement of your goals.

Family and Friends

Your family and friends make up a large part of your life. Although your interactions with them tend to be positive, they can still have some undesirable results on your academic progress. Excessive chatting and outings can take up valuable study time, distract you from your focus, and discourage you from following through with your goals. Conflicts may arise between what your family and friends want from you and what you demand of yourself. Instead of running into social problems in the future, you can plan ahead in order to prevent such situations from arising. Although you will maintain your independence, you want those around you to understand and to be considerate of what you are doing. Your family and friends care about you and want you to do well, so they should be accepting and proud of your efforts. Likewise, you will want to be appreciative of anything they do in order to help you.

You are developing your self-dependency and are devoted to reaching your goals. This demands your time. There will be occasions when you will not be able to do an errand for your mother because you will need that time to study for your English test the next day, instances when you will not be able to meet your best friend for smoothies because you will be staying after school to work on a report in the library, and so on. Your schoolwork does not give you an excuse to disobey your parents or to bail on friends; you need to plan ahead and negotiate around such conflicts. This way, you will avoid potential misunderstandings of your academic agenda and prevent the hurt feelings that can result.

Think about any time-consuming activities in which your family or friends expect you to take part, such as if you and your sibling alternate nights doing the dinner dishes. Consider if it were your evening to clean, but you had so much to do that you felt you couldn't spare the extra half an hour the dishwashing would take you. Your sibling would of course not appreciate having to do the dishes on your night, and it could lead to a fight or hurt feelings between the two of you. It is therefore a good idea to let your sibling and the rest of your family know ahead of time about your time limitations and other commitments and to create a plan for such circumstances. The other individuals involved will then be more understanding when conflicts do arise. You may decide, for instance, to plan that on busy nights your sibling will do your cleaning with the knowledge that you will make up his or her chores on another day. In this way, planning

> *Parents can come off as really annoying at times. However, often they may simply be expressing their interest and support for your academic endeavors. If your parents ask about your school day, don't make the mistake of blowing them off. Instead, give them a synopsis, a brief summary, of what you did in each class and of any new assignments you were given. The overview can be beneficial for both you and them.*

ahead prevents trouble and will allow you to focus on your work, and not on conflict resolution, when time is tight.

I recommend you go ahead and call a family meeting to plan for the future. Talk to your close friends over lunch or whenever you have a private moment with them. You probably will prefer to speak with your close ones individually, but you may decide to do so in a group all at once. Remember, these actions will only take a bit of your time now and will save you a lot of time and hassle in the future. Who knows, you may even inspire some of your friends or siblings to care more about their own academics and to join with you on the road to success!

On the following page is a helpful list of ideas you may choose to mention when you talk to your friends and family. Say the items you think most appropriate. You can write down some of these ideas ahead of time so that you will be sure to cover all you want to say. There is also room on the list for you to add your own items that you feel are important to address. The degree to which you use the items on this list depends on the magnitude of your goal, the levels of flexibility and understanding that your family and friends currently have, and the level that you feel they need to have.

Watch out for saboteurs! Saboteurs are people who try to sabotage and hinder your steps to success. These people will tell you that you are working yourself too hard, not relaxing enough, not giving enough of your time to others, or that you are being an over-achiever. Ignore this friend, classmate, sibling, troublemaker, or whoever else it may be. The individual is most likely jealous and attempting to prevent your success. Also, the saboteur may be worried that as you become more successful you may not like him or her anymore. Recognize this when it happens and deal with it as you see fit, but don't give in. Keep away from saboteurs, and be aware of their hurtful aims.

Friend and Family Considerations

- Explain to them how important they are to you and how their support would benefit you.

- They can affect your feelings toward schoolwork, and you would like them to positively reinforce you.

- You are letting them know of your new commitments ahead of time in order to keep things running smoothly for both you and them.

- This is a serious effort on your part to achieve your goals, and you are putting your time, attention, and effort into doing so.

- You are committed to the fact that, in general, your schoolwork must take priority over other activities.

- It is best to develop a plan so that when your schedules do conflict, you can amicably work around it.

- You will still have time for them, of which you will definitely want to make use.

- You usually will not have time for excessive chatter and gossip during the school week, including at home, on the phone, and over instant messenger.

- You will need time to yourself to think and do your work independently.

- You soon will be making a schedule that includes your academic commitments and other activities. You can include time to spend with friends and family on your schedule.

- _____
  _____

- _____
  _____

- _____
  _____

- _____
  _____

You must not allow yourself to be distracted from your focus. Furthermore, you want to stay on good terms with those around you. Make sure to pay attention to your friends' and family members' responses to what you have to say. If any issues arise in your conversation, go ahead and take action by planning for the future and for any conflicts that could result. Do this before more time goes by. On a night when you have a lot of work to do and not much time in which to do it, you won't have time to be thinking up compromises or giving explanations.

> "Home is not where you live, but where they understand you."
> -Christian Morgenstern, German author and poet

Networking

As I grow older, I realize more and more how important our connections with other people are. Today's world more than ever before allows for quick and easy communication. You can use this to your advantage. Every acquaintance, friend, and contact you make provides you with another person who may be able to help you towards your goal. When needed, you can rely on someone in your communication base to give you helpful information and insight into the topic at hand. Such a network lends valuable connections and assistance in the academic world.

There are people you currently know, or whom you can get to know, who can assist you in doing well in school. There are other students who put a lot of effort into their schoolwork and are trying to get or keep their grades up, just like you. It is good to have people like this around you for several reasons.   Firstly, it is a reminder to you that you are not the only one committed to working hard and doing well in school. Many students feel more comfortable knowing that there are other students close by also committed to their studies. Secondly, such a network can be motivational because you may become a little competitive. Competition gives you a boost of motivation to work hard. You know how that goes—*If she was able to score in the 90s, then I definitely can, too!* Of course, you don't want to try to bring others down in order to build yourself up. That is not how to succeed, and no one is looking to network with someone like that. Some light competition, however, can give you a little pep in your studies. Thirdly, success-minded students can be of assistance in your academics. Although you want to be self-reliant, at some point you may need something from another student. For example, if you missed a point your teacher made during class, you would want to get the information from a classmate later so that you could add it to your notes. It is good to be acquainted with those students upon whom you can depend to be a reliable source of information. Fourthly, such success-minded students may often prove to be good friends. They, just like you, are trying to do well in school. To this end, they will understand that you are often busy with your schoolwork. They also have school as a priority in their lives and understand the importance of doing well. In addition to this, if your school has its classes segregated according to academic challenge, you will probably find you end up with the same high-reaching students in most of your classes. It will of course be more enjoyable for you to be friends with several of your classmates. These are some of the direct advantages of building an academic network, and you will realize many more indirect benefits as you progress.

To some people, the idea of networking seems intimidating—you need to search for useful connections, bridge new friendships, and open yourself up to many new people. Networking, however, is not as difficult and technical as it may sound. In fact, it can be quite fun, and there are many ways in which you can gain these helpful connections.

> *If you ever feel nervous asking someone you don't know a question, take a moment to ask yourself what the worst that could happen is. Usually, it would be for the individual to say "I don't know." When I was in high school, several times students who I barely knew called me with questions related to schoolwork, and of course I was glad to help them and to get to know them better.*

First of all, it almost always works to be upfront about your aims. Talk to some of those high-achievers who seem nice, and let them know about your commitment to doing better in school. Ask if you can call them in case you have a question, and make sure to exchange phone numbers with each of them. Keep track of those numbers; they will come in use! Likewise, let these students know that you are glad for them to call you if they ever need anything. Networking is a two-way street.

To get acquainted with the other students, try sitting near them in class. You can chat with them in homeroom or before class begins. In the lunchroom, give your peers a smile and a quick *"hey!"* when you see them. They will understand these small gestures to mean that you like them. Quite simply, people like to be around those who like them.

Therefore, they will return the sentiment.

Extracurricular activities are a goldmine for building network connections. Not only do these activities provide you with countless opportunities to meet new people and make new friends, they also allow you to become involved in something that interests you or that you enjoy doing. Take advantage of your time in high school by participating in clubs, sports teams, and events that peak your interest. When choosing what activity to involve yourself in, consider if it is an activity you will enjoy doing, if it is something that will make your resume stand out, or if it will be a way for you to meet or become closer with some of your peers. Your time is valuable, and you want to enjoy yourself and have fun while doing well in school.

Finally, if you ever do find yourself without a network and in need, just ask someone who seems reliable to you. Get right to the topic of what your question is and see if the individual can help. Often, you will meet people with whom you may have otherwise never spoken.

When you enter the world of academic success, the social question as to whether you really know someone well enough to contact them about schoolwork is of diminished importance. What matters is doing well in school, and successful students know that, so feel free to talk to whomever you need for assistance. Try not to feel awkward about talking to a student whom you do not know very well. The worst that could happen is that the other student may not know the answer. That's not so bad, is it? And if a student you didn't know very well contacted you for some help, wouldn't you be glad to help them if you could? Learn from and share with the people in your network, and look to make new friends and acquaintances whenever you can.

Choosing Classes and Teachers

Schools often offer various types and levels of classes and teachers from which you can choose. Most likely, some classes are known to be more difficult, while others have a reputation for being easier. The same is often true for teachers as well. Many students blindly choose their classes and end up taking a class that they do not enjoy or that they find overly difficult. Luckily, you can avoid this situation by doing some research about the classes and teachers at your school. Your class selection is an important decision, as it dictates what you will be doing next semester and, consequently, how well you will do. Note that school course selection processes vary widely. Therefore, apply the following guidelines as closely as you can with your school's specific process.

Planning your class schedule takes serious time and thought. When it comes time to decide your schedule for the next semester, look over the list of what your school is offering. Jot down a list of any classes or teachers you are interested in taking, and start using your network. Call up friends who have taken the courses on your list and ask for their thoughts and opinions. The students who know the information you need will usually be in a higher grade than you due to the fact that they have taken more classes and have already completed the grade level at which you are now.

For each class, you need to find out whether it is a class in which, or a teacher with which, you can do well without going through unreasonable measures. To find this out, try asking some of the following questions.

About the class:

- On what information does the class focus? *(Ask yourself if this is something that is of interest to you and in which you will be motivated to do well.)*

- Approximately how much time daily do you have to spend preparing for the class and doing assignments?

- How much homework is given? Is it difficult, and is it graded?

- Are the tests and quizzes difficult, and how often are they given?

- What makes up your grade for the class (homework, papers, tests, class participation, projects, etc.)?

- _____

  _____

- _____

  _____

  _____

- _____

  _____

About the teacher:

- Does the teacher keep the class interesting?

- Does the teacher take and answer questions during class?

- Is the teacher nice and easy to talk to?

- Is the teacher generally available to provide extra help if needed?

- _____

  _____

- _____

  _____

- _____

  _____

Considering that class selection processes can vary, you may have other questions pertinent to the classes or teachers at your school. Write these in on the blank lines included with the questions listed above. This way, you will have these ideas recorded for future class registrations as well.

In addition to talking to students, you may also want to try asking some of the adults at your school for their opinions. School guidance counselors can often give you feedback on classes and teachers. The guidance office is regularly visited by stressed-out or angry students who want to talk about a particular problematic class. This office also sees the grades that students receive in their classes. With this knowledge, guidance counselors can give you some insight into choosing appropriate classes and teachers.

Once, I was standing in the guidance office at my high school, waiting for my counselor to become available. While I was there, I heard one secretary say to the other, "Did you see the grades for the yearbook class? That teacher is so demanding. Literally half the students failed!" I made a mental note to limit my yearbook involvement to club activities and not to take the class.

One word of caution: at times, others will offer you inaccurate or incomplete advice. Be aware of this, and consider whether or not the individual with whom you speak is truly knowledgeable and looking out for your best interests. Remember that simply because one student found a class overly difficult does not mean that it will be difficult for you, and vice versa is true for if a student found a class to be particularly easy. Simply put, you want to be self-reliant, and take your own thoughts and feelings on the matter as the final word.

In addition to guidance counselors, teachers you have had and are friendly with may be able to advise you as to which classes would be good for you. The advantage in this is that your past teachers know how you work and what you can do. They may be able to give you the best advice on which classes you would do well in and enjoy, especially now that you are improving your academic capabilities. These teachers also interact with the other teachers on a personal level, so they may have a strong understanding of the real personality of the teachers from which you are choosing. Even if you are not close with a specific teacher, I still encourage you to talk to him or her if you think it can help. Many teachers will be pleased you asked them and will give you thoughtful advice.

Be sure to check **Sites for Students** in the appendix. It lists useful internet sites, including some that allow you to read comments written by other students about their experiences with specific teachers at your school.

You want to succeed in school and get higher grades. This means that you need to take classes in which you will be able to get the marks you desire. Jot down the answers you get to your questions and look for those classes that cover topics you will be interested in and that will keep you motivated in the course. You are also looking for a class that doesn't demand unreasonable amounts of preparation each night; *maximum* average assigned preparation time per class should be about an hour and a half. This includes the time it takes to do homework and any assigned readings. Besides doing what the class asks of you, you will be doing some of your own necessary preparations for each class. If the class assignments take too long, you won't have time to do your own, extra preparation to ensure that you do well. If by your own judgment you deem a class worth taking even though it has a high preparation time, I recommend you go for it, as long as you feel that your other reasons for taking the class outweigh the difficulties it presents.

There are some additional factors you may want to consider with regards to the information you find out about your potential classes. As far as homework goes, a class that gives graded homework would probably be preferable for you. With graded homework, you know you can get an *A* on every assignment because you will have available all of the resources you need to answer the questions correctly. Furthermore, homework is work that is beneficial for you to do and that you need to do anyway, so it is usually a plus to get credit for it. Just be sure to find out how much time it takes to complete the homework adequately in order to do well. Graded homework turns into a negative factor if it takes up too much of your time.

The benefits of graded class participation can vary between individuals. Some students are naturally more comfortable being involved in class discussions. If you are not one of these students, you may still benefit from graded class participation. Being able to speak in front of others is a great skill to have. Also, as you will soon learn, you want to participate often in class in order to maintain interest, show involvement, and keep yourself from getting lost. Since it is beneficial for you to participate in class, a class that grades you on your participation could help you by giving you the motivation to do so. If, however, you do not feel you can participate well enough to earn a good grade, you will want to avoid such classes.

Finally, it is best to avoid classes with exceedingly difficult graded assignments, namely tests. You plan to be totally prepared for everything and anything your teacher may throw at you. However, if a certain teacher is known for giving trick-filled tests, it could hinder your progress even if you know all of the information really being asked. You want to avoid classes that could trip you up even when you truly are doing everything you can to learn the material.

If you do end up taking a tricky class or a class with some other problematic characteristic, don't let it stress you out. It is good that you found out ahead of time about the hard parts of the class so that you will be even better prepared. Furthermore, we will soon go over the steps you need to take in order to do well in tough and tricky classes.

As far as teachers go, you want to have a teacher from whom you will be comfortable learning. A good teacher makes a conscious effort to keep his or her pupils motivated and interested in the material presented. Moreover, a good teacher is generally willing to take and answer questions during class. The learning process is based on you being able to think about and understand the information you are given. If you are confused about something, you need to be able to get clarification so that you can digest the new information. When you are in class, the teacher is generally the best source of information. It makes things more difficult when your teacher is not willing or is unable to answer questions.

Along these same lines, your teacher's personality may also play a role in your decision. You want to be able to have positive feelings towards and to get along with your teacher. If for some reason this is not an option, it should not be too much of a problem as long as you are able to learn from and be graded fairly by him or her.

Lastly, being self-dependent you are not planning to need extra assistance from your teachers. But it is nice to have the option available to you. If, for instance, you do fall behind in class, it would be beneficial for you to have a teacher willing to meet with and help you. Furthermore, some teachers hold after-school review sessions before tests. Often, these teachers will review key ideas on which they are planning to test you. If you are lucky enough to find a teacher that offers thorough test review sessions, take him or her. When you know the test material well, you also know you will do well on the test.

Choose the classes in and the teachers with which you are most likely to meet your goals. In addition to this, make sure to take your subjects in the right combination. You don't want to be stuck with all hard classes for one semester and then only easy ones for another. Have a rough idea of what you will be taking in the future and try to plan for it. Besides balancing easy and hard classes, you may also consider balancing your classes in terms of very interesting with not-so-interesting, time-consuming with not time-consuming, fun with frustrating, and any other combination that is important to you.

By putting your network to use and making well thought-out decisions, you will end up with teachers and classes that will propel you towards your goal. You will know what to expect going into your new classes, and you will have an enjoyable semester due to your thoughtful planning.

SUMMARY: PREPARING YOUR LIFE

- Inform those close to you about what you are undertaking, what it means to you, and what it entails.

- Plan how you will handle any commitments that may conflict with your academic agenda.

- Networking will make it easier for you to do well in school. Benefits include: more academic support and motivation, possible assistance from others, and new friends.

- To create a network, reach out to others by sitting near them in class, giving a quick smile and saying *"hey"*, or speaking with them at shared extracurricular activities.

- If you ever find yourself in need of help and without a network to turn to, simply approach whomever you think can best assist you.

- Use the past experiences of others to make your academic schedule a surefire success. Turn to your network, other students, teachers, or guidance counselors to gain others' opinions and knowledge. Remember to take the information with a grain of salt, considering ideas of what makes a class easy and interesting or tough and boring can vary from person to person.

- Purposefully select those classes that are best suited for your personal goals, and remember to consider the long-term consequences of the way in which you plan your current course schedule.

3. *Organizing for Success*

As you have probably realized by now, succeeding in school will take time and work, both of which are items we do not like to dole out in large quantities. Fortunately, strategic organizational techniques will allow you to avoid wasting energy, time, and effort. When you are well-organized, you can work more efficiently, expeditiously, and easily.

Successful organization also includes thoughtful rationing of your time. Therefore, in this section you will develop your time management skills. We will discuss how to schedule your life so that you can complete your schoolwork and other obligations while still having some time for yourself. Finally, we will go over the importance of those zzz's!

Tools for School

At school, you want to have the necessary materials readily available so that you can easily stay organized, take notes, collect handouts, and so on. Most students actually end up buying too many school supplies and are left lugging around superfluous items. You want to keep the clutter of school supplies to a minimum. If your teacher asks you to have specific items for his or her class, and if you will actually get use out of these items, it makes sense to have them. In general, however, all you need are the simple supplies we will discuss below.

> *"Simplicity is the ultimate sophistication."*
>
> -Leonardo da Vinci

Your main tool for school is a plain three-ring binder. The one inch or one and one-half inch size typically works well for up to eight classes. You want a durable binder that will last through the entire school year. For our purposes, a simple binder is best; you don't need one that has a padded zip case around it. Make sure the binder you purchase has pockets, preferably one on both the front and rear flaps.

At all times, your binder will contain several specific items. Snapped into the rings you will have a flat, zip-up pencil pouch. The pencil pouch should have holes through which the binder rings can fit. Try to get a pouch made out of a tough fabric or plastic so that it can securely hold your writing utensils while maintaining flexibility and durability. It will also be helpful to you if it has a plastic or mesh see-through section so that you will be able to see exactly what you have inside without having to open the pouch. It is best to have the pouch in front of all other items snapped into your three-ring so that you will always have easy access to your writing supplies.

Directly behind your pencil pouch, include about twenty pages of loose-leaf paper. College-ruled paper tends to make your work look neater because it leaves less room for sloppy writing. Choose wide-ruled only if you feel more comfortable using it.

In addition to your binder, there are several other important items you will want to have at school. Students often want to know the time during a lecture or test, and it is therefore very useful to have a wristwatch, preferably a digital one so that you can see the numbers at a glance. Usually, inexpensive athletic watches are well-suited for this purpose because they feature the time and date as well as stopwatch and alarm functions. In addition to having a reliable watch, you should buy some attractive pens and pencils for yourself. It is more fun to take notes with a pen that has a cool grip or with a neat-looking mechanical pencil. If you think this shouldn't make any difference in how well you do in school, then you are right. However, just give it a try. You will most likely find that doing so helps you to keep your spirits up and to stay interested in what you are working on. Take one or two each of your pens and pencils to school every day, and bring a separate eraser along as well. If your teacher requires you to write in pen and you are prone to being messy and needing to erase, go for erasable pens. The pens you write with normally should be blue or black, and your writing pencils should be normal carbon graphite, not colored. In addition, you will want to have a highlighter and several colored pens that write in visible colors. You might want to try one of those pens that can write in multiple colors depending on which tab you click. We will discuss how to use these when we go over strategies for effective note-taking, outlining, and class preparation.

Finally, you need to have a well-organized homework planner. The planner should provide each weekday with its own box and a generous amount of writing room; sections for Saturday and Sunday are preferable as well. Generally, you will be using your planner to keep track of everyday assignments, long-term projects, social events and other responsibilities. We will discuss how to use your homework planner in the **Doing**

Your Homework section. Your planner should be durable so that it will last you the school year and survive your daily trips between school, class, and home. At the same time, you do not want your planner to be so large as to be burdensome to carry around with you. Look for a planner with small overall dimensions but with a cover made of a tough material, such as thick plastic.

Here is a list of the items you need for school.

Tools for School

- 1-inch or 1½-inch durable, pocketed binder
- Flat cloth/plastic pencil pouch fitted for binder
- Loose-leaf paper (preferably college-ruled)
- Athletic watch with stopwatch function
- Attractive pens and pencils; optional: erasable pens
- Separate eraser
- Colored pens and a highlighter
- Homework planner
- Optional: reading glasses and/or distance glasses
- _____
- _____
- _____
- _____

School supplies are meant to help you do well in school. If you can think of any other items you will need at school, add them to the list above. Having the necessary tools for school is crucial to your success. If what you need for your classes changes at any point, get whatever new tools you may need as soon as possible. When you are busy tackling your schoolwork, you will want to have your full academic arsenal at the ready.

Tools for Home

As we discussed in the previous section, in school you need relatively few items on hand. This is partly due to the fact that you will have most of your school supply inventory at home, where you will be doing the majority of your academic preparation. There you will have everything you need available to you, and you will not have to worry about carrying anything around with you such as you do at school. Instead, you will have the ease and convenience of your own customized study spot.

Your study spot is a comfortable workstation you will set up at home. There, you will keep all of the materials demanded by your classes. There should be no *box* temptations in the immediate area nor people running in and out of the room. When working at your study spot, you may also want to shut off your cell phone and any other items that could disturb or distract you.

Your will store all of your old notes, hand-outs, tests, and other assignments at your study spot. Your study spot is where you will be doing serious studying and work, and at times you will want to look back at your old notes to compare information or to look up something you have forgotten. Having these resources readily available to you will make your work easier and can even make the difference between a B and an A in the long run. The easy access you will have to this ample information will lead you to look up and review items you may have otherwise ignored and forgotten.

If possible, arrange to have your own desk with drawers and a big well-lit open space on which to work. Most students like to make their study spot in their bedrooms, where they can easily shut the door and thus keep the room calm and quiet. Optimally, items in your drawers or on your desk should include those items listed on the following page.

Tools for Home

- Pens and pencils
- Colored pens
- Highlighters
- Erasers and whiteout
- Sheets of three-hole-punched, college-ruled paper
- Several 2" binders
- Tabbed dividers for the binders
- Ruler
- Calculator
- Stapler and staples
- Paper clips
- Hole puncher
- Dictionary
- Thesaurus
- Wall calendar
- Scissors
- Tape
- Manila folders
- To-do list
- Clock
- Optional: chalkboard or dry erase board; tack board
- Optional: reading glasses
- _____
- _____
- _____

Here's an idea:

If your lined paper is prone to tearing, try using reinforced paper or buying reinforcement stickers (rings that you place around the holes). These items are commonly available at discount and office supply stores.

The utility of most of these items is self-evident. However, there are a few that we will discuss in further detail.

It is important that you give some time and thought to creating a functional study spot. Your first step is to make sure that your surroundings are clean and organized. Empty out any old garbage or non-school-related supplies from your desk drawers. These items could get in your way, and they give an overall sense of disorganization. When it comes to your schoolwork, you want to be able to work methodically and with order. Starting from this clean foundation, you can begin to add your study tools. Remember when deciding where to place these items that you want to keep your work surface open, clear, and available for doing your schoolwork.

Your study spot is where you will work every day when you get home from school. There, you will sit down and organize any new material you received during the day. At your study spot, you will need to have several large binders, sectioned with tabbed dividers labeled for each of your classes. This way, you won't have to carry around old papers and notes at school. You will instead have them all at home, systematically filed away in your large at-home binder. Whenever you need to find a handout you used in class, or when you need to get out all of your notes to study for a test, you will know exactly where to look. I find the best size for these binders is two inches; a two-inch binder can usually hold about three or four classes worth of material per semester. Try to select binders that have pockets on the front and rear flaps so that you will have extra storage space available to you. In addition to your large binders, you will want to have a few labeled manila folders around in case you ever do not want to hole punch an item or in case want to keep it separate from the rest of the items in your binder. At the end of the school year, you can put all of the filled binders and folders away, maybe in your closet if there is not enough room in your desk, so that you will have the information clearly labeled, organized, and readily available to you should you need to look up something relevant to future coursework.

You are probably also wondering to what the *to-do list* above is referring. Your to-do list is basically a small notepad, or even just a couple of pieces of paper, on which you can jot down anything you need. We will discuss how to use it later on in **Scheduling**. The to-do list is a very useful item to have and you will definitely want to have it available to you at your study spot.

During the school year, you will take on different projects and have to commit to various events both in and out of school. To keep tabs on your responsibilities, hang up a large wall calendar near your study spot. On this calendar, write everything except for your daily short-term homework assignments. This includes items such as long-term projects, special events, and any new activities that may arise. This way you will be able to see at a glance everything that you have coming up. Also, you will be able to easily add new events as they arise. If possible, you may prefer to get a wall calendar with room for notes at the bottom, so that you can write down any relevant information about your scheduled events.

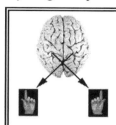

For the most part, your right brain controls the left side of your body, and your left brain controls the right side of your body. Try this: When you use the computer, use your non-dominant hand to control the mouse. It may seem awkward at first, but keep with it. Experts believe that introducing mental stimulation such as this to the other side of your brain may improve overall brain function and ward of mental diseases such as Alzheimer's.

Optimally, it would also be nice to have a chalkboard or dry-erase board on which you can write anything you want. It doesn't have to be big; mine is only about the size of an 8x11" piece of paper. You can prop it up on your disk or stick it to the wall. Some students also like to have a board on which they can tack up papers associated with the work they're doing. Often chalkboards and dry-erase boards come with a section onto which you can tack papers. I do not have one of these, so when I want to have an important paper nearby, I simply tape it onto the wall or onto the side of my desk. Another helpful idea is to have a pad of sticky-notes nearby. On these, you can jot little reminders or whatever else you may need to have sticking around your study spot.

On a final note, we should talk about having a computer. Many teachers expect their students to have access to a computer and printer. If you do not, you can usually arrange to use one at your school or local public library. If you have your own computer, or if you share one with your family, you may want to consider arranging your study spot so that the computer is nearby. This way, whenever you need to check something on the computer, it will not be far off. It is most convenient, of course, to have your own laptop, which you generally should leave at your study spot. If you do not have a laptop, or even if you do, I recommend you get a USB flash drive. This device allows you to save your documents from one computer onto it, and then later to open those same documents and work on a different computer. Therefore, even if you do not have your own laptop, you will have the flexibility of being able to easily transport your files from one location to another.

Since you are going to be spending so much time at your study spot, you should also consider adding some other items in order to ensure you are at ease there. Firstly, your chair should be comfortable; you shouldn't have to lean over too much to read and write. Also, there needs to be enough electric light around your study spot so that even when it gets dark outside you will not have to strain your eyes to read. Several other accommodations I find useful include having a light jacket or blanket nearby in case you get cold, a box of tissues for colds, allergies, and spills, and a capped water bottle in case you get thirsty. If there are any other items you would like to have in your study spot, add them to the list of tools for home on page 37. For instance, I periodically get backaches, so I would add a pillow that I could use to support my lower back.

> *In addition to a USB drive, you can transport electronic documents via e-mail attachments. However, the internet can distort documents, and some computers do not even have internet access or the correct programs to open certain files. Therefore, it is still to your advantage to have your own USB device.*

Many students find it comforting to do their schoolwork while listening to music. I sometimes like to do this as well. If you enjoy listening to music while you work, then by all means you should do so. First, however, there are a couple of items of which you should be aware. For one, music can serve as a distraction, especially when it has lyrics. Students often find themselves singing along or daydreaming about the song instead of completing their assignments. I have a friend who does not study to music with lyrics because she can't help but sing along. In such cases, it may help you to listen only to instrumental music, or to avoid listening to music all together. Another problem with listening to music is that some students make it into a box activity. They start playing with settings and switching back and forth between different songs instead of focusing on their work. To avoid this, two things should be done. First of all, and most importantly, you should make a conscious effort not to fidget with your music paraphernalia. Secondly, try creating your own personal album containing all of the songs you would like to listen to while studying. This way, it will not be necessary to flip back and forth between songs. To make your own soundtrack, you can record good songs off the radio onto a tape, write songs from your computer onto CDs, or make a separate playlist of study songs on your MP3 player. Be sure to choose songs that will not distract you and that are conducive to studying. As long as you follow these principles, playing music while you work can be soothing. Music sets a soothing rhythm for you to work to and drowns out distracting background noises.

> *Some studies suggest that music may impact our intelligence and productivity. For example:*
> - *Students who listened to 10 minutes of Mozart prior to taking the SAT had higher scores than students who weren't exposed to music (University of California).*
> - *People who listened to light classical music for 90 minutes while editing a manuscript increased accuracy by 21% (University of Washington).*

We have so far discussed the best items for you to have at school and at home. Now would also be a good time for you to think of any special considerations you may need regarding your schoolwork. For example, if your back aches from carrying heavy books back and forth between school and home, you need to be proactive in trying to find a solution. In this instance, you could sign out two textbooks from your classes that have heavy textbooks. You could tell your teachers that you have back problems and that you need to have one book for school and another one for home in order not to strain yourself. The extra books were just going to sit around anyway, so your teacher should be glad to let you borrow one. It is important to do what you can to ensure that you are as comfortable as possible doing your school work at home, at school, and at any place in between.

Time Management

Good time management skills allow you to have time for all of your various activities and responsibilities. One important skill you want to have is the ability to plan and schedule everything that you need to do. A good schedule takes into account all of your commitments, whether they be daily or long term, school or nonschool related. Your goal regarding scheduling is to have your

> *You may also find these pointers to be useful in other areas of your life. It never hurts to have more time!*

days filled with getting done what you want and need to do and to have plenty of time to eat, sleep, and relax.

Before we get into making your actual schedule, let's go over some time management basics. First of all, *activities generally end up taking longer than people expect them to take.* When considering how long you should expect an event to last, compare it to any similar events that you attended in the past. Decide if there are any reasons that this occasion would take more or less time, and adjust accordingly. This includes time allowance for any problems that may occur, such as a poor internet connection or getting stuck behind a slow driver on your way somewhere. If you have to travel for a commitment, remember to include commute and parking in your time estimate.

Another common pitfall for students is *procrastination*—avoiding the very work they need to be doing. It takes diligence and assertiveness to avoid this trap. You need to keep an eye out for and avoid opportunities to procrastinate. People often find themselves making good excuse after good excuse to put off a project, but this can be detrimental to their success in school. *If you have something you need to get done for school, get working on it as soon as you can.* If you delay, you will have to cram in your work at the last minute, lowering the quality of your work, decreasing the understanding you gain from the project, and causing your teacher to give you a lower grade. Also, you won't be able to enjoy the time you procrastinate away because you will have the pressure of completing your project hanging over your head. At its extreme, procrastination can even cause you to fail to finish the assignment, quite a catastrophe for any success-minded student. If, on the other hand, one follows this simple principle, as you will, and avoids procrastination, it will result in the completion of the project in a timely manner, a better understanding of the material, a higher grade, and more enjoyable free time.

You will be making your schedule with the goal of succeeding in school. Therefore, completing all of your schoolwork and academic commitments should take priority over other activities. To make sure all of the necessary items are included in your day, you will use your daily homework planner. We will go into greater detail about how to use your planner when we discuss homework. What is important concerning your time management skills is to *make a habit of consulting your planner every day*, especially when making up your daily schedule. Also, since academic success is the focus of your schedule, you want to avoid taking too much time for extraneous activities on school nights. The majority of your free time will be when you do not have much left to do for your classes, often on weekends or during school breaks and vacations.

Sometimes, you will end up making an unexpected break in your schedule. It may be because you decide to go to a movie at the last minute or because some free baseball tickets suddenly became available to you. Whatever the case may be, when making the decision to depart from your schedule, take it seriously. Make sure that doing the new activity is really worth putting off what you had planned to do. Along with this, *consider how and when you will be able to make up the interrupted activity.* If you decide it is possible to make this interruption in your schedule, then commit yourself to making up the work that you are momentarily skipping. Before leaving, set a time at which you will end your break and return to your original plan. Usually, it is best to restart your schedule from where you left off. There may be projects farther down on your schedule which you will no longer have time for and which you will need to arrange to complete somehow. Set a location and time at which you will be able to do the missed work. Try to be creative and to improvise. Will you have time later in the evening? Can you do the work in the car on the way to the new event? Think about all of the possible opportunities in which you can do your work, such as on your bus ride to school, during lunch, between classes, in study hall or recess, or whenever else you are able to squeeze in some extra work time. Obviously, the ideal is to stick to your schedule and to avoid having to do your work late at night or on the bus. However, if the situation calls for it, you have it in you to do what it takes.

To be time efficient, you want to put all of your time to use. If you want, you can also integrate into your schedule those same empty time slots in which you can do missed work. If you have a quiz after your third period class, for example, you can plan to use the time between your first few classes to review last minute concepts you need to go over. There are many little blocks of time available to students throughout the day, but most people do not acknowledge them and spend the time idly. If you put to use all your small and obscure free time slots, it will add up to one productive larger block of time. Keep an eye out for any time in which you can complete your work. If your teacher ends class early, start on the homework right away so you will have less to do later. If you finish the work while still in class, you won't even have to bring your textbook home.

The more efficiently you use your time, the more quality free time you will have for yourself.

You should also *take into account the effect other people may have on your time*. Don't plan to study at a location where you will have constant distractions. Look for places in which you can work undisturbed. Otherwise, the time you expect a project to take may be greatly extended.

Finally, good time management skills involve *letting others know about your plans*. When your family and peers have an idea of how your schedule goes, they will be more amenable to accommodating your needs and will be more understanding during your busier times. By planning your free time, you will be able to give adequate attention to your studies and to others. It just won't be at the same time.

Time Management Skills Summary
- ➤ *Allow enough time for activities to take a little longer than expected.*
- ➤ *Avoid procrastination by starting on projects right away; a small step in the right direction is infinitely better than no step at all.*
- ➤ *Prioritize your schedule with the completion of your schoolwork and academic commitments.*
- ➤ *If you decide to interrupt your schedule, commit yourself to making up your work in a timely manner.*
- ➤ *Look for any time you can put to use; that way you will have more time to play!*
- ➤ *Avoid working in distracting surroundings.*
- ➤ *Involve your peers and family in your schedule.*

The Race to Bed

Many high-achieving students take a big hit in the sleep department. By planning your work well and scheduling a bedtime, you can avoid this unhealthy routine. Sleep is important for your overall comfort, health, and success in school.

With respect to your health, sleep plays many important roles. For one, growth hormone and a hormone named leptin rise to their peaks during sleep. Health professionals believe growth may be stunted in those young individuals who receive inadequate shut-eye. In addition to this, researchers have found that these hormonal changes can cause those who do not get enough sleep to eat more throughout the day.

Regarding schoolwork, scientists have also found that while we sleep, our brains review and organize the information that we learned throughout the day. Clearly, getting inadequate sleep is not only a matter of temporary discomfort, as so many believe, but rather it can actually harm you and your progress in school. To keep yourself healthy, strong, and clear-headed, you need to get enough sleep.

As with most matters, you need to set an achievable goal in order to ensure your success. In this case, your goal is your bedtime. Instead of simply setting a time, though, define to yourself what that bedtime means. Are you going to be in bed, asleep, or just starting to prepare for bed at that time? I suggest you plan a firm time at which you will begin getting ready for bed, and an approximate time at which you plan to be in bed and asleep. Make sure to plan your evening carefully so that you will be asleep by your goal time. Some important items to get done in the evening include packing your book bag, planning your lunch for the following day, and picking out your clothes. This routine will give you a head start in the morning so that you can squeeze in a bit more shut-eye.

> *Dr. Richard D. Simon Jr. specializes in sleep medicine at Providence St. Mary Medical Center. He says people have a group of cells in their brains that explain their biological clocks. "These cells are programmed to turn on for about 16 hours a day, and they turn off for about eight hours at night usually," Dr. Simon says. "Those cells stimulate us to stay awake. The longer we are awake, the more the brain develops a need to sleep. So the longer I am awake, the sleepier, if you will, my brain gets."*

Your bedtime needs to allow you to have enough sleep before you have to wake up for school. Most researchers have found that eight is the magic number of hours. Eight hours allows your hormones to cycle naturally and generally will leave you feeling refreshed. People vary in their sleep needs, however. Some feel they need only seven hours, while others cannot do without at least nine. One of my friends is unique in that she only needs about five hours to feel well-rested; very rarely does someone require so few hours of sleep. As for me, I find the typical eight hour rule does quite well, although I definitely wouldn't mind getting more! You have been living with yourself long enough to know how much sleep you need to perform well. If you haven't really noticed how many hours that is, try eight and see how that leaves you.

Next, consider when you will need to wake up in the morning in order to allow yourself enough time to eat breakfast and get to school on time. Studies have shown that

It is estimated that 25% of American youths don't eat breakfast in the mornings. This is unfortunate, as breakfast really does provide fuel for the day. A study in the journal Pediatrics found that teenagers who regularly ate breakfast weighed less, exercised more, and generally had healthier diets than their peers who didn't eat breakfast. The report found that those teens who skipped breakfast weighed about five pounds more than those who regularly had a morning meal.

eating breakfast can improve your overall nutrition intake, concentration, and ability to control your weight. Most nutritionists recommend a filling breakfast high in protein and fiber, such as whole grain oatmeal with blueberries and a touch of cream or a veggie-packed omelet. After you have decided on an appropriate wake-up time, subtract eight hours from it (or whatever your magic number may be) and determine the time by which you need to be asleep. Then, figure out when you will need to start getting ready for bed in order to be sure you are asleep by then. Aim to be in bed at least fifteen minutes before you want to be asleep. This will allow you a little extra preparation time and time to fall asleep.

People often make getting ready for bed take much longer than necessary. For that reason, think of your preparation time as a race—a race to get to bed, that is. Nick reasoned out his bedtime routine on the following page. After considering his thoughts and your particular needs, you will have the chance to write out your own routine as well.

Nick's Bedtime Plan

School starts at 8:15AM, and the bus picks me up from home at 7:30AM. If I jump up at 7:00AM, I can make the bus in time. As soon as I get up, I'll use the bathroom, get dressed in my preplanned outfit, eat breakfast, brush my teeth, grab my bag, and run out to the bus stop. Like most people, I need at least eight hours of sleep, so I will need to be fast asleep by 11PM. I'll aim to be in bed by 10:45PM, especially considering that things always take longer than people expect them to take. To keep my morning routine short, I need to plan ahead the evening before. At 10PM, I will stop whatever I am doing and pack my schoolbag for the next day, making sure to pack my lunch money. I will also shower, get in my bed clothes, and pick out my outfit for the next day. Then, I'll go ahead and do any last minute tasks and wish everyone good night before I go to bed. At 10:45PM, I will get into bed and turn off the lights.

Start: 10:00PM

Checkpoint: 10:45PM

Finish: 11:00PM

It will be beneficial for you to think about and write down your evening routine as Nick did. Doing the same activity each evening will help your body to recognize that you will soon be going to bed, in turn making it easier for you to fall asleep. In addition to this, you generally won't forget and leave out an important step in your routine since you will be used to doing the same tasks nightly. For Nick, once it hits 10PM he knows exactly what he has to do and he does it. He also made a good choice to take his shower in the evening. The temperature change of a warm shower has been shown to help people fall

Barbara S. Natoli, executive director of Applied Behavioral Associates, LLC, recommends sticking to a consistent bedtime routine as well as minimizing highly stimulating or stressful activities at least one hour prior to bedtime.

asleep. Also, with an evening shower, you won't have to worry about waiting for the bus on a freezing cold day with a wet head of hair.

On the lines below, there is space for you to write out your personal routine. Afterwards, don't forget to set your own start, checkpoint, and finish times for your race to bed!

My Bedtime Plan

_____

_____

_____

_____

_____

_____

_____

_____

_____

_____

_____

Start: _____

Checkpoint: _____

Finish: _____

You want to stick with this plan as best you can. There will inevitably be times at which you will have to stray some from your routine. On school nights, this will most often be because you need to finish a school assignment and therefore won't be able to start getting ready for bed on time. At that time, you will have to decide between going to bed late or waking up early in order to do the assigned work. In general, I recommend the former, and I will tell you why. Firstly, the majority of pre-teens, teenagers, and young adults are not "early to bed, early to rise" people. Studies have shown that at that age our brains are naturally wired to prefer staying up later than waking up earlier. Secondly, if you plan to wake up early, you may accidentally not allow enough time to finish the assignment before you have to leave for school. Waking up early also poses the opposite risk: that you wake up so early that you allow too much time to do the work and thus end up awake when you could have been asleep. By doing the assignment the night before, you ensure that it will be completed in its entirety in the necessary amount of time. Furthermore, it is beneficial for you to sleep after completing assignments and studying because it gives your brain the opportunity to reiterate and review the new information while you sleep. If, however, you ultimately find that waking up earlier is better for you than staying up later, then do so; do whatever is best for *you*.

> *Many yoga practitioners integrate the calming tripartite breath into their routines. To try it yourself, lie down on your back with your legs comfortably extended and your arms by your sides, palms facing up. Close your eyes and rest for a moment. Through your nose, draw a deep breath down into your abdomen and feel your abdomen rise in response. Continue to inhale as the air fills your lungs and ribcage area and travels up to your collar bone. Hold for a moment if you choose, and then slowly exhale out through your nose, releasing the air from top to bottom, sequentially from your collarbone area, ribcage, and abdomen.*

If you didn't get enough sleep during the week, it is a good idea to sleep in a little on the weekend. Just be careful not to stray too far from your school day schedule; don't go to bed extremely late or sleep in until the afternoon. Your body tries to program itself to a regular sleep schedule, and you don't want to disrupt this process on the weekend. Plan not to sleep more than an hour or so past your regular wake up time. You want to get adequate and enjoyable sleep without messing up your body's biological clock. This way, you won't have difficulty sticking to your academic schedule on weekdays.

Another disrupting sleep favorite of some students is napping during the day. While a small few find naps to be invigorating, the vast majority of teenagers find them to be a waste of time. Your body expects to be awake during the day and asleep at night, and therefore it usually won't be ready to fall asleep in the daytime. If you try to take a nap, you may have difficulty falling asleep, and, even if you do eventually fall asleep, you run the risk of not waking when you planned to; the snooze button, or just shutting the alarm clock off, is a huge temptation. When you wake up, your body may feel groggy and confused as to whether it is supposed to be asleep or awake. For these reasons, napping generally detracts from students' collective nighttime sleep time. Furthermore, if your body becomes used to napping, you may start to feel sluggish when you are trying to do work during the day, causing you to feel the need to nap when you would not have otherwise. If you feel fatigued and cannot continue your work without a nap, it is reasonable to make a conscious decision to take one. Just make sure to consider the cons mentioned above first, and don't let it become a habit.

Along these same lines, always go to sleep at night when it comes time. On a school night when you don't have a heavy workload and don't need to stay up past your bedtime, don't. Even if you are not tired, you need to get in bed and relax in order to prepare your body and mind to go to sleep. Otherwise, you will be exhausted in the morning. It will be difficult to manage your time and schoolwork well when your body and mind are trying to make up for lost sleep.

To avoid being kept awake at bedtime, experts recommend avoiding caffeine for at least six hours before bed. Six hours is the amount of time it takes for half of the caffeine to leave your body. This compound will keep you awake even when you are thoroughly fatigued.

If you ever need a stimulant to keep yourself awake, though, caffeine may be useful. Do be careful not to overuse caffeine as it may be harmful in massive quantities. Tea is by far my favorite and the healthiest for your body because of its high antioxidant content and more moderate caffeine level. In the mornings, some factors that may help to wake you up include eating a nutritious breakfast, being exposed to sunlight for at least ten minutes, having a cup of tea or coffee, or sipping a glass of chilled water.

Time management skills include knowing how to keep your mind and body alert so that you can work efficiently. You can achieve this by getting adequate sleep.

Scheduling

Your schedule is an application of your time management skills. It makes your tasks more manageable because it lays out your commitments on paper and tells you what you have to do and when you have to do it. Every day you will quickly make a schedule fitted to what you have to accomplish on that particular day. The events on your schedule are based in part on your homework planner, wall calendar, and to-do list. By following your well-thought out schedule, you position yourself for success.

After school every day, you should allow yourself a little break. During this break, you can do some nonschool-related activities, such as read a newspaper or magazine, exercise, or have a snack. A small break after school gives you some time to relax and reflect on your day before going back to work. Try to keep the break relatively short, although it will vary in length depending on what you do during it. After your break it will be time for you to make your schedule. On days I didn't have an extracurricular activity to go to after school, I would come home and go jogging for about half an hour. Then I would sit down and have a snack while writing out my schedule for the day.

In your homework planner, which we will discuss more in the section on **Doing Your Homework**, you will list your classes and their corresponding daily assignments. You will always list your classes in the same order, preferably in the order of your classes during the day. When it comes time to write your schedule, think about each of your classes in that order so that you do not forget to include one. Since your schedule is comprised in large part of what is written in your homework planner, you may be able to complete your list by simply adding to what is already written in your planner. In general, though, getting out a fresh sheet of paper for your list will allow you plenty of room to add whatever you would like. On your schedule, you will list for each class: everything you were assigned that day, anything you need to do for a long-term project, and any other items you think necessary for that class. In later sections, we will discuss what further considerations you should make at this point.

At the end of your list, add on any items from your to-do list and any other commitments you may have for that particular day, such as doing your laundry, washing the dishes, playing with your siblings, etc. Your to-do list is an important part of ensuring you do well in school, particularly because it helps you to recognize the commitments you have and because it decreases the likelihood that you will forget about one of your responsibilities. Let's take a moment to talk about how to put this handy little tool to work for you.

Whether you are at home, at school, or in the grocery store, you always want to have your to-do list easily accessible to you. It doesn't have to be anything special. It can be a blank piece of notebook paper, a tiny notepad, or even the back of a piece of scrap paper. Make sure your to-do list is clearly labeled and dated at the top so that you do not mistake it for anything else. You can carry it around folded up in your back jean pocket, book bag, purse, wallet, sweatshirt pouch, or wherever else it will be convenient to you.

On this list, you should jot down any commitments to which you need to attend besides your daily school assignments. More than simply being a list of items you need to do, this paper should also have on it any reminders you may need or ideas you have. For instance, if you are eating lunch at school and suddenly think of a good topic for your research paper, put it down on your list. If your friend gives you his e-mail address, jot it down. Everything you want written down should go on your to-do list. When it comes time to write your schedule, be sure to include all applicable items from your to-do list.

Of course, simply writing the list without taking action on its comments won't do you much good. For instance, you may need to file your friend's e-mail address into your address book or to write the research topic idea on a paper in the English section of your binder as soon as you get home. You don't want to end up with lots of old to-do lists with little reminders and facts you wanted to keep around. Something needs to be done to get each and every item on your to-do list accomplished. Whenever you complete a commitment on your list or get the idea or information you jotted on it stored in its proper place, such as on your daily schedule, clearly check the item off your to-do list. Start a new list once you complete your current one. You don't want your list to become too cluttered or illegible.

Your to-do list is an asset to your success. One reason students often fall behind in school is due to the fact that they overlook details when it comes to correctly completing assignments. They may forget the good ideas they thought of earlier in the day or may fail to fulfill an obligation they had. Your to-do list helps you to easily and conveniently keep track of everything you have to do, so you know that you will get it done. Review your to-do list throughout the day and make sure to include the items on it in your daily schedule. Most importantly, tailor your list and method of using it so that it best suits you. The list is there to help you, not to put you up to extra secretarial work.

Nick's schedule that he made in his homework planner is shown on page 54; your schedule should be organized in a similar fashion to his. As you can see by looking at Nick's sample, he wrote his schedule in order of his classes. Since chemistry is Nick's first period class every day, he listed it first. Public speaking is Nick's last period class, so he listed that course last. Schools vary in the way they organize their classes, however, you should be able to find some way in which to organize your list so that it follows the real order of your classes throughout the day. You don't want to accidentally leave out an entire class.

Remember to add your nonacademic tasks, even the trivial ones, such as taking out the garbage, to the end of your list, as these too will take up your time. Also, specify on your schedule exactly what each item entails. Instead of writing *do math homework*, specify the page numbers and exercises for the assignment. That way, you only have to look at your schedule, and you will not need to refer back to your homework planner for the actual assignment (if you are making your schedule on a separate sheet of paper). Make sure to think through *all* of your courses, commitments, and assignments so that you do not leave something out.

Nick's Tuesday Schedule

Chemistry

       9-Do worksheet 11.2

       10-Read textbook pp. 124-128

       11-Answer questions on p. 129

       8-Review today's notes

English

       16-Research Paper: write thesis statement and look for more sources

Geometry

       17-Do textbook p.83, #11-29 odd

       18-Review today's notes and yesterday's notes

Phys Ed

       20-Bring new gym clothes

US History

       12-Read and outline pp. 203-215

       13-Test Friday: start reviewing notes and chapter summaries

Spanish

       6-Do green packet

       7-Do worksheet *El/La*

       4-List new vocabulary words from today's lesson

       5-Review new vocabulary words

Public Speaking

       19-Brain storm ideas for speech next Tuesday

To-Do List

       1-Write thank-you card to Grandma

       2-RSVP for Randy's party

Other

       3-Clean kitchen before Mom gets home

       14-Take out trash

       15-Play catch with little brother

       √ -Go running

After you have listed everything you need to do on your schedule, it is time for you to decide the order in which to carry out your many tasks. In general, it is best to do all the assignments for a particular class consecutively so that you can take advantage of the fact that you are in the *frame of mind* that the specific subject requires. Also, you generally will want to get the shortest assignments out of the way first. If you do a very long assignment first, it could spill over into time that was meant to be used for doing smaller assignments. At the same time, you of course wouldn't want to end up not working on an important term project because you were busy doing all the smaller, less important items on your schedule. You will need to get to the big projects at some point. In the section on **Doing Your Homework**, you will learn to break these big projects into more convenient, smaller assignments. At this point, you need to know for your schedule that the most important thing with big projects is to go ahead and get started. Don't put a project off because it is not due until weeks from now. You need to break the project down, as we will discuss later on, and start working on it right away.

The order of your schedule needs to be logical. This simply means that, for example, if you are assigned a worksheet on what you did in class, you will need to review your notes before you do the worksheet. Reviewing your notes needs to get the number directly preceding the one you assign to doing the worksheet. Another consideration you need to be aware of is if the order is feasible for the other aspects of your life. If you need to wait for your dad to get home from work so he can take you to the library, then getting sources for your paper at the library cannot be the first thing you do in the afternoon. On this same point, if you want to play catch with your little brother, it still needs to be light outside, so it can't be the last thing on your list. Make sure the order also fits into your personal habits as best it can. If you look, Nick made packing his clothes for gym the last item on his list. This is because he always packs his bags right before he goes to bed, so while he is doing that he will pack his gym bag as well. Think carefully about the order in which you should do your work, and then, after writing out all of your obligations, give a number to each assignment for its proper place on the schedule.

Write the appropriate number on the left of each listed item. Nick has done this on his schedule as well. Remember, of course, that your focus is on your schoolwork, and you therefore want to give priority to completing your schoolwork before any other activities or assignments. If you have very small things you need to take care of that are not school-related; it may make sense to do them first. You don't want to interrupt your schedule later on in order to do them. Larger items that are not school-related should only be included as high priority if you are sure time permits them. On days when I had a ton of work to do, I didn't have time to go running, or I went for a much shorter run. Also, although Nick already went running before writing out his schedule, he included it anyway so that at the end of the day he could see all he had accomplished. I recommend you do the same so that you can keep tabs on how efficiently you are spending your time.

Some people like to rewrite their lists in order at this point. However, doing so is generally a waste of time. All you really need to do once you have made your schedule is to get started on task #1.

Breaking up long stretches of schoolwork with several minutes of other activities has been shown to improve one's mood and efficiency while working.

If you feel the need, you can take a small break every now and then throughout the day. This will give your mind some relief and keep you from getting bored or distracted. Your breaks should usually be about ten minutes. The frequency of your breaks depends on your preferences and workload. If you only have a couple of assignments, you may not need a break, while if you have a ton of work to do you won't have much time for breaks. In general, a short break between every other subject works well. For example, Nick would do his Spanish and Chemistry homework and then take a short break before beginning US History. A break is a good time to get a snack, take a quick walk outside, rest your eyes from the computer screen, or read an interesting article out of one of your magazines. Your breaks are actually meant to save you time by enabling you to keep up your efficiency and good spirits.

Remember, your free time is dictated by your schedule and your focus. If your favorite television show is on at nine at night and you have completed everything on your schedule by then, that's great! You can go watch your show with the knowledge that you are doing everything necessary to succeed in school. If, however, you have not completed your schedule, you may under no circumstances watch your show. Usually, you can find some way to handle the situation. In this particular case you could ask a friend or family member to record it for you. You shouldn't record it yourself because you have no time for any distractions until you have completed your schedule, and box-related activities, such as recording something on the television, often take up more time than they should. You may be able to watch the show later in the evening if doing so doesn't cut into your scheduled bedtime, or you can watch it another day or on the weekend.

There will be times, however, in which you won't be able to make up for the missed event. At such times, you will have to sacrifice fun things in order to complete your schedule. You cannot allow a little distraction like watching television or going to an unscheduled event take you off your path to success. The opportunity cost for doing something in place of your scheduled work is far too great. To succeed in school you simply cannot live only for the moment. You need to work for the future so that you will have a great future. Learn to like doing what you know to be right and best for yourself.

SUMMARY: ORGANIZING FOR SUCCESS

- Get only the school supplies that you need.

- Make a customized study spot for yourself equipped with your home tools and any other accommodations you may need. Your study spot should be box-free (except for a nearby computer, if available).

- Review the time management skills summary presented on page 44.

- The priority of your schedule needs to be completing your schoolwork and academic commitments.

- If you must break from your schedule during the day, recognize it and commit to ending the activity and returning to complete your work by a specific time.

- Look at all the small time spots you have available throughout your day and put them to use. Consider your bus ride to school, lunchtime, time between classes, any free periods or study halls, homeroom, if a teacher lets you out of class early, etc.

- Schedule some time for your family and friends, and let them know your plans.

- Define a bedtime for yourself, and aim to get at least eight hours of sleep a night.

- On weekends, keep a sleep schedule similar to your weekday one.

- When you get home from school each day, take a short break and write out your schedule.

- Don't let anything sidetrack you from your path to success. Don't succumb to the small distractions of the moment; work for a successful future!

4. In the Classroom

∎∎

Your actions in the classroom determine in large part the grade you will receive for a particular course. Unlike your study materials, the classroom presents you with a dynamic environment involving constant interchange between yourself, your teacher, and your peers. There is a lot for you to keep track of, and it is essential to your success that you use classroom time to your advantage. As you will find in this chapter, the many different aspects of classroom activity fall into three main categories. We will now go over the techniques and strategies that will enable you to master and manage these three facets in order to propel you towards your goals. You will also learn how to efficiently and effectively take notes in class.

Classroom Behavior

You will be able to work more efficiently in the classroom once you understand the role your teachers and peers play there. The three main aspects of the classroom are not difficult to master, as long as you know how to do it. You need to be able to:

1. Present yourself well to your peers,
2. Get the most possible out of every class, and
3. Be on good terms with your teacher.

The aura you create around yourself in the classroom affects how well you learn the material presented to you and says a lot about you to the teacher. Some teachers tell you class participation makes up a portion of your grade, and others don't. However, know that even when you are not technically being graded on class participation, it is your teacher who will be deciding your final grade in the course. Generally, your teacher can always push up your grade a notch if he or she feels you deserve it.

> *"Nothing succeeds like the appearance of success."*
>
> *– Christopher Lasch, American historian and social critic*

❖ **Your *Peer Review***

For starters, you want to appear to others as if you are focused on doing well in class. For one thing, it's true, and, additionally, giving such an appearance shows others to treat and respect you as an academically minded student. It also helps you to feel as such. To be seen as a good student, follow the guidelines below.

1. *Always come to class*. Don't skip class because then you will miss vital information and show your teacher and peers disinterest and a lack of effort on your part. Along with this, make a conscious effort to be a couple of minutes early to every class and to be prepared with everything you need. This will show others that you care about the class, and it will give you time to prepare your materials and to get in the right frame of mind before the teacher begins the lesson.

2. *In the classroom, sit up front and near your teacher so that you are clearly in the teacher's line of sight*. You want to show everyone who you are, i.e. someone who is focusing on the class and on what the teacher is saying. Being in such a prominent spot will put you in the classroom spotlight, a great spot for avoiding distractions and building a connection with your teacher.

3. *Make a conscious effort to participate*. If you have a good point to make, you want to say it aloud and contribute your thoughts to the classroom discussion. In this way, you will show others that you have been listening and that you have an understanding of the topics being discussed. Make sure to speak up as soon as you can because you want to contribute your idea before the discussion changes direction or before you lose the opportunity to speak. If you are still developing your own ideas, you may decide to first listen to the questions and comments of your classmates before speaking up. This latter option gives you the opportunity to hear what others have to say, and listening to their ideas may help you to further develop any ideas or to answer any questions of your own. It will also give you time to think over what you want to say. Contributing questions or comments to the classroom discussion will benefit both your and your peers' appreciation for the course material.

4. *Allow your classmates to recognize the dependable hard-working student that you are.* Your peers may sometimes ask you questions or ask for advice with their work. As long as they don't take up an inconsiderate amount of your time, it is to your benefit to help them. Doing so reinforces the new ideas for you and helps out others, too. You will gain the reputation in class as someone who *gets it* and shares with others, and it will motivate you and help you to succeed in the course.

❖ **The Real Rehearsal**

You can use classroom participation to your advantage, whether the participation is graded or not. Participation shows others how seriously you take the material and helps you to be involved with and understand the lesson better. Before you come to class, set goals as to how much you will say and what you will say. For instance, you can decide to get called on at least three times during the period, to comment at least once on each poem your teacher goes over in English class, to ask at least two questions that day, etc. Be careful; if you do not have a goal, you may end up saying nothing.

In my AP English in high school, I walked in every day with a participation goal. Sometimes I knew exactly what my comments and questions would be before walking through the door, other times I only had a goal as to how much I would say. Most importantly, I decided not to let the fear of sounding dumb get in my way. After all, participation requires that you participate, not that you are totally correct or that everyone agrees with you all the time. Many students avoid participation because of fear, but the truth is that everybody makes mistakes and it is nothing to be ashamed of, especially in the classroom environment. When participation is making up part of your grade, the only mistake you can make is not to participate. Say anything intelligent and relevant that comes to you, particularly if it is in response to another student's ideas. Plan ahead of time; discuss it with others before class; do what you need to so that you will be able to participate. Your participation and ideas contribute to the class.

At times, students may fall flat in their participation. They may lose sight of the topic being discussed or they may not have been paying attention to what the speaker was saying. While this happens to everyone, there are ways to avoid this problem. Try to look at the speaker's face at all times. Doing so helps you to pay attention and to be conscious of what the speaker is saying. Looking at the speaker gives you the added benefit of seeing the facial expressions and body language that go along with the ideas being spoken, enabling you to get a better sense of how the speaker feels about what he is saying. While someone is speaking, it is also important to involve your mind actively. Ask yourself what the speaker's main point is and why he is making that point. Think about if you have anything to ask or to contribute further towards the discussion. This way, you will not zone out, you will learn and remember information better, and you will be more likely to have ideas and things to say of your own. Look at the person who is speaking and mentally and verbally involve yourself so as to benefit your peer performance and improve your concentration.

> *One helpful way to gain a better understanding if you are confused by something is to ask your teacher to give you an example applying the concept. Seeing how the concept applies to matters to which you can relate will help you to better understand and remember it.*

If you ever fall off track and have trouble understanding the material being presented in class, then simply raise your hand. Your school supplies you with a teacher so that you can interact, raise questions and new ideas, and so on. You can't simply ask your textbook for guidance or for the answers to your questions, but you can do so with your teacher. Be specific with your question. Before you ask the question, go over in your mind what you already know just in case you can answer it yourself. If you decide to ask your teacher, it is helpful to start your question with a quick summary of your understanding of the concept you are learning so that your teacher can correct any misunderstandings you may have underlying your question. After giving the quick summary, and gaining your teacher's consent as to if it is correct, ask your question as concisely as possible. Giving the summary of what you know has the added benefit of once again emphasizing that you have been paying attention and are actively involved in the class.

Being that it is school, it is inevitable that you will get bored in class at times (just kidding, right?). Pertinent to this are two ideas. Firstly, even if it is boring, you don't want to miss any information that could have an impact on your grade. If you are supposed to be learning something, you need to pay attention to it no matter what. When your mind wanders and you start thinking about something besides what you are learning at the moment, gently pull your focus back to the classroom. Banish any of those distracting little thoughts from your head. If it is something you want to dwell more on later, then jot it down on your handy dandy to-do list. Secondly, if your class is slow and boring and the material being presented won't have any effect on your grade (such as a teacher going over the quiz you just aced), then this is free academic time. If you want, and if you are very careful, you may use this time to review notes, organize papers, write down assignments, work on projects for another class, etc. Only make sure that you don't do the other work in a way that will attract the attention of others; it is usually disrespectful to show that you are giving anything less than 100% of your attention to the present class. Doing work for one class in a different class is another reason why it can be helpful to have one binder that holds the material for all of your classes. In that way, you will always have the necessary work available to you. By getting the work done now, you will have more time for play later.

❖ **Talking with Your Teacher**

Your interactions with your teacher can play a large role in your grade and success in class. If your teacher likes you, he or she will often be more likely to help you out and to think of you positively when it comes time to decide your final grade. This is clearly someone with whom it would behoove you to have a positive relationship.

First, recognize that your teacher is a person, too. Surprisingly, students often forget this most obvious fact. Your teacher stands in front of a classroom full of students every day. It can be nerve-wracking to have twenty or so sets of eyes constantly watching everything you do, and it can be tedious to have to teach the same material over and over again to different classes. Because of this, your teacher will slip up at times. Your teacher may forget to say or may purposely skip something he really should have taught. For you to succeed, you need to get the necessary information from your teacher without coming off as a pest. Furthermore, you must truly want to learn the material; if all you want is a good grade your teacher will pick that up and it will count against you. While maintaining the student-teacher relationship, try to interact with your teacher on a person-to-person level.

When you are sitting in class, especially in the spotlight, keep your eyes on your teacher except when someone else is speaking. Remember to sit up straight. It is good for your posture, keeps you feeling more alert, and sends a message to your teacher that *you*

According to a 2003 report published in Nature Biotechnology, researchers discovered a tiny bacterium capable of converting simple sugars into electricity with 81 percent efficiency.

are interested in what he or she is saying. To further show your interest in the class, keep an active face. This means to listen to and respond appropriately to what your teacher is saying. Something funny? Smile and laugh. Something interesting? Raise your eyebrows; look more intense. If you don't get why this matters, take a second to think about it. Imagine if you were teaching a class of students about a new invention, such as a battery that runs on sugar rather than electricity, and no one even acknowledged your interest nor showed any of his or her own. To say the least, it would be disheartening and put a damper on the lesson. Furthermore, it would imply that the students either did not understand or were not paying attention to the lesson. Therefore, engage yourself; respond appropriately to emotional cues and build common ground with your teacher. Sometimes, you can simply give a small reassuring smile to show that you appreciate the lesson. It will be more gratifying for you to learn from a person with whom you can relate rather than to feel as if you are being preached at by a largely unfamiliar character in the classroom.

Also, take note of your teacher's personal characteristics. Does he focus on the specifics or on broader points? Does he want you to memorize facts or to learn to apply concepts to novel problems? There are so many possible variances. You want to be able to put yourself in your teacher's frame of mind so that you can figure out what questions he may expect you to be able answer and how you will have to answer them. To do well on any test, it is always helpful to know the individual who wrote and who will grade the test.

Furthermore, if you ever have trouble in class or have difficulty preparing for a test, know that you can approach your teacher for advice. Your teacher may have noticed particular spots that have been problematic for you on assignments. With his insights, he should be able to guide you in the right direction to improve your class performance. You can also ask if there are any extra credit opportunities available, as we will discuss in **Asking for Extras**.

Your teacher may offer his time to any students who need help. Teachers often make lunch and after school time slots available for students to come for extra help. If you are having trouble doing well in a class or if you have any specific questions, this may prove very helpful to you. Look for such chances, and request them if necessary. Just like when asking a question during class, you want to have your problems defined when you go to your teacher for help. Seeing and getting to know your teachers outside of and after class builds a bridge of communication between you and them.

A great subject to look for extra help in is writing. If your teacher ever offers to look over a written assignment before its due date, you should take advantage of it. Whatever corrections or suggestions your teacher makes on a written rough draft will be of great help to you when you have to revise the paper. Writing assignments can be very subjective in terms of grading. You may write a great paper on one teacher's terms, but the same paper may appear average to another teacher. Therefore, always try to write your rough draft for a written assignment as soon as possible. Then, if or when your teacher offers to look over rough drafts, you will have yours ready. It will also give you more time to edit the rough draft and will allow you to include your teacher's revisions in it.

Besides making sure to stay on your teacher's good side, be proactive about avoiding going over to his or her other side. This of course includes simple manners, such as not talking to other students when you should be paying attention. In addition to this, many teachers feel threatened or embarrassed when someone else corrects them. If you ever think your teacher made a mistake or is wrong about a particular item, or if your teacher ever makes statements contradicting what you have read from a reliable source, broach the subject carefully. In general, you should maintain respect and presume that your teacher is correct in his assessment. This is also a good idea since the misunderstanding could very well be on your end! Simply tell your teacher you do not understand how he came to his conclusion and then explain how you came to a different conclusion of your own. Your teacher will either recognize that you are in fact correct, or he will help you if you are mistaken.

Remember, your teacher cares about your performance in school and should be willing to help you get back on track if you need help. It is worth it for you to make an extra effort to maintain a positive relationship with him or her.

Taking Notes

Notes are the tell-all of how well a student works in the classroom. It often seems to me as if we are tested on our note-taking ability more than anything else. What we choose to write down becomes what we study and, in turn, what we know when test time comes around. The purpose of this section is to teach you how to filter for the information you need to ace the test and how to organize your notes to get the necessary information written down most efficiently.

❖ **What to Write**

You cannot write down everything your teacher says. Not only is it not possible, it is also not practical. The more notes you have, the longer it will take you to review them later. You want to write down all of the information you need without writing down anything superfluous. In essence, you need to know what to ignore, what to write down, and how to do it quickly and in an organized fashion.

Your notes need to reflect the fact that you are actively listening to and understanding what your teacher is saying, not that you are writing down everything you possibly can. You want your notes to include important ideas and their supporting details, as well as any key terms or phrases that may pop up on a test. To help you recognize significant items, consider the criteria listed below.

Include an item in your notes if:

- You are told it will be on the test
- Your teacher raises his voice or sounds excited about it
- The teacher repeats it
- The teacher writes, circles, or underlines it on the board
- The teacher says it is an important study topic
- It is advice about how to study a particular topic
- It is a good sample test question
- It is mentioned on the course syllabus
- It is a central idea that connects to previous lessons, helping to support a general theme and to maintain the continuity of the course

- It is information related to the test/assignment: due date, format, topics it will cover, applicable textbook readings, length, *any* hints, etc.

- It is instructions for homework (write it directly onto your homework, if possible)

- It is something your teacher discusses that is not in the section of the textbook you are currently covering

- It is part of a numbered list

- It is part of a diagram or chart

- It is a new or unfamiliar term

Note that while this list is very specific, most of the bullets fall under the main categories of including new or especially important information and assignment details. Do not memorize this list; rather, take the time to understand why these items are significant. Your goal is to keep insignificant items out of your notes and to recognize what is important for you to take note of.

There are also several other helpful cues that will tell you when you should write something down. For one, teachers tend to use the beginning and end of class to summarize what you should be getting from the lesson and any important points. What your teacher says at these times will help clarify the main idea for you. You may also want to write down a little interesting fact every now and then. For example, your teacher may mention a cool way in which what you are learning explains a phenomenon in your everyday life. Although you often will not be tested on such information, you can still jot down the idea in your notes. Later, when you are reviewing your notes, the information will serve as a little reminder that what you are studying actually has a purpose outside of simply being schoolwork. It is such a relief when I study to see a little blurb that is interesting and that I don't have to memorize. It helps to keep my attitude positive and my spirits up.

Ultimately, you want to have in your notes all of the information that you need to know to get high grades. When your teacher is teaching you something, ask yourself what main point he is trying to get across. You want to understand the general idea and how the specific points you are learning apply to that broader picture. Take this questioning a step further in class. Analyze your teacher's approach to the material. Try to pretend you are your teacher, teaching the information to a classroom full of students. From his or her vantage point, decide what matters most about the topic. If you understand your teacher's angle on the subject matter, you can better anticipate what he will focus on for your next test.

Sometimes, your teacher will ask the class open questions about what you are learning. Write these questions down! They could be similar to, or may even be, the very questions you will have to answer on your next test. And, if you are unable to tell what your teacher thinks is important, you always have the option of asking. Usually, you want to assume that the information your teacher gives you is pertinent test material. However, if he diverges from the topic you are studying or goes extremely in depth for one particular item, you can ask if you are responsible for knowing all that material for the test. Try to avoid asking this question in general as your teacher can take it to mean that you are not interested in the material, but only in your grade. Even if it is true to an extent, most teachers would prefer you take an interest in the course material and learning process as well.

❖ **How to Write It**

Class notes are simply a list of organized information. Your handwriting needs to be legible so you can read what you write, and the order of your notes has to make sense so that you can understand the information while reviewing it. To help keep your notes neat, write only on the front of each page. Writing on the back may become messy because your writing will be etched on the opposite side of the page and your notes on the next page may smear some on the back of the prior page.

On your first day of classes, write the class title on your first page of notes as well as the date including the year. Any time you complete a full page of notes, you will bring it home to add to your at-home binder. If your last page of notes from class is not entirely full, you will bring that page with you to class the following day and continue from where you left off. When you continue, simply add the day's date of the next set of notes in the margin of your new starting point. For example, if on *9/28* you took two and a half pages of notes in Geometry, you would bring the first two pages home and add them to your at-home binder; we will discuss this binder shortly in **Reviewing Your**

Notes. The final half page of notes you would bring back to Geometry class the following day. Then, beginning directly beneath your last line of notes from the day before, you would write *9/29* in the margin and continue your notes as usual. This method allows you to maintain continuity and limits the number of pages you will have to keep track of and review.

❖ **General Note-taking Format**

The most basic way of taking notes is the general note-taking format. I find this often to be the most efficient method. It conforms to just about any subject matter, and it allows you to arrange information in an organized fashion. This method is most simply an organized list of information. A bullet (●) marks the start of a new general topic of study. The points of information directly beneath the bullet are marked with dashes (—). When your teacher eventually switches to a different subject, put down another bullet (●) with the new topic title. Make sure to leave the margin empty; we will discuss its uses soon. Nick used this model to take some chemistry notes. Look at his example on the following page to gain a better understanding of how to apply the general note-taking format.

- *Matter*
  - *matter: anything that takes up space and has mass*
  - *matter consists of chemical elements in pure form and in combinations called compounds*
  - *element: substance that cannot be broken down to other substances by chemical reactions*
  - *every element has a symbol*
  - *compound: substance consisting of two or more elements combined in a fixed ratio*
    - *has characteristics beyond those of its combined elements*
- *Structure of an Atom*
  - *atom: the smallest unit of matter that still retains the properties of an element*
  - *atoms are symbolized with same abbreviations used for the element composed of those atoms*
  - *'H' symbolizes both the element hydrogen and a single hydrogen atom*
  - *atoms are composed of even smaller matter called subatomic particles: neutrons, protons, and electrons*
  - *neutrons and protons are densely packed in the nucleus*
  - *the electrons form a cloud around the nucleus*
- *CONT: Matter*

If your teacher ends up switching back to a previous bullet, you can add the notes underneath the original bullet if there is room available. If not, however, do not try to squeeze anything in; this only leads to messy notes and illegible writing. Instead, create a new bullet at whatever point you are at in your notes and write *CONT:* before you write the exact same bullet title again. This is shown in Nick's notes. His teacher first spoke about matter, then about the structure of an atom, and then his teacher switched back to the topic of matter. It is important to include *CONT:* so that when you review your notes, you will be sure to find the original bullet instead of accidentally missing the first bullet on a particular subject.

It is always okay and even preferable to include pictures and diagrams in your notes, especially if they will help you to understand the written information at a later time. Also, underneath any dash, you can indent and create another dash (—) for information pertaining specifically to the dash directly above. As you see, Nick did this in his notes to include further details about compounds. Only use this indented dash if you feel what you will write there will actually help you to study better. Your regular dashes should contain all information relevant to the main, broad topic of the bullet. In general, you will use the indented dash to include a more obscure piece of information or a specific example relevant to the non-indented dash on the preceding line.

It all comes down to what you feel is the best way to take notes for your particular class, learning style, and teacher. You want to organize and distinguish the main points and their characteristics from much smaller details while maintaining a systematic format. This form of note-taking is great because it is efficient and allows for easy organization.

Notice that in his notes, Nick underlined certain words. These words are some of the key terms he needs to know for class. Whenever your teacher defines a new word related to the subject you are studying, you should write down the definition and underline the new word. Your teacher expects you to know this word and its meaning well.

Underlining the new word will help it to stand out to you when you review your notes. You want to make any particularly important sections of your notes stand out as

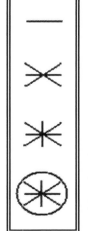

well. If your teacher emphasizes a point, or tells you to memorize something, you need to mark it. There are several ways to do so. If there is a particular important point you listed next to a dash, make the dash into a large asterisk by drawing an X and a vertical line through it. Put a thick circle around the asterisk so that you do not miss it while reviewing. For items you need to know well, such as key concepts, formulas, or definitions, you can draw a box around the relevant information. Finally, if there is a piece of information you need to memorize, write *MEM* in the margin directly adjacent to the information. You don't want to overlook something you must memorize.

❖   **Comparing and Contrasting: T-Charts and Venn Diagrams**

If your teacher compares and contrasts items in class, you can organize your notes in a different format to make the points of comparison more clear. The first method is called a T-chart. A T-chart is a simple chart including a heading and its details in a vertical column. The next column over contains the other item being compared. Each row of the T-chart considers a different characteristic of the topics being compared. For instance, in the following sample T-chart, the third row presents the relative strengths of each format type. You may sometimes need to skip lines on one side of the chart in order to keep the information in the columns properly paired. Look at the sample T-chart below to see how it is organized and how the details are paired to match up in rows.

T-Chart: Comparison of T-charts and Venn diagrams

T-Charts	Venn Diagrams
Neatly organized	Tend to get messy
Used for comparing and contrasting	Used for comparing and contrasting
Show direct contrast between certain characteristics	Show overlapping similarities between topics
Drawn by making a big lower case 't', with parallel horizontal lines drawn across it	Drawn with two or more large overlapping circles
Numerous topics can be compared	Can only neatly handle up to three topics

Another possibility for comparing and contrasting is the Venn diagram, which has the added benefit of allowing you to clearly identify characteristics shared by two or more topics. The Venn diagram literally shows the overlap between the topics. It is made up of two or more large circles. If you have more than two topics to deal with, you can draw more than two overlapping circles, as shown on the following page. One problem with Venn diagrams is that they tend to get a little messy; you may run out of room in the section for shared characteristics. See the examples on the following page, as they show this problem even though there is only one overlapping characteristic given.

Venn Diagram: Comparison of T-charts and Venn diagrams

T-charts   Venn diagrams

- Neatly organized
- Show direct contrast between certain characteristics
- Numerous topics can be compared
- Drawn by making a big lower case 't', with parallel horizontal lines drawn across it

Used for comparing and contrasting

- Tend to get messy
- Show overlapping similarities between topics
- Can only neatly handle up to three topics
- Drawn with two or more large overlapping circles

3-Topic Venn Diagram   4-Topic Venn Diagram

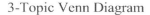
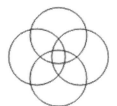

Remember to always label your T-chart or Venn diagram with a title so that you will know what it is about with a quick glance. When deciding which comparison method to use, focus on which one will allow you to understand the information best at a later time. Generally, T-charts are better suited for highlighting contrasting characteristics, while Venn diagrams stress the similarities of the topics being compared.

Usually, you will stick with the general note-taking method. At times, however, you will want to use one of the comparison methods explained above or one of several other note-taking methods explained in the following pages. You may use these styles during class or reformat your notes to one of these styles at a later time. Some students find that it is easier for them to remember their notes when the information is arranged in a more content-specific format. While looking over these methods, make sure you understand how to apply them and when it will be beneficial to use them.

❖ **The Pyramid Method**

The pyramid format is excellent for two main uses. For one, the pyramid can display *hierarchical* systems, with the peak representing the highest power and the rows below representing those systems that work under or that make up the foundation of that higher power. For example, in the pyramid format, the president of the United States would make up the top tip of the pyramid while the large base would represent the American people. The levels in between the two would be filled stepwise with the various political powers responsible for legislation and judicial review. When two political bodies have equal power, they share the same level in the pyramid. In addition to showing hierarchy, the pyramid structure can indicate quantity. Shown on the following page is the older version of the USDA-approved food pyramid, which highlights this second use. Used this way, the pyramid clearly displays the *quantities* allotted for different food types. The foods that are supposed to be consumed in the greatest quantities are placed in the large bottom area of the pyramid, while those that should be eaten sparingly are close to the pyramid's narrow peak. Those items that require similar quantities, such as fruits and vegetables, are split on the same level; here a slightly larger area is given to vegetables since they require slightly more servings per day.

As with all note-taking formats, always title your pyramid so that you know its topic at a glance. The pyramid method is great for arranging information either by hierarchical organization or quantitative differences. You will therefore most often find this format to be helpful in classes related to government, history, biology, and other similar subjects or topics.

The Pyramid Method

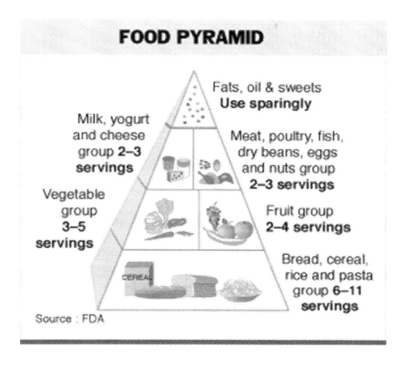

❖ **The Cycle Diagram**

Cycle diagrams are advantageous to use when dealing with a topic that is continuous. This format clearly shows cause and effect and shows how a specific step can cause a chain reaction that leads right back to the original event. I have used the water cycle as an example. Precipitation falls to and collects on the ground. Water on the earth evaporates into the sky and condenses into little water droplets. These droplets collectively form clouds, which eventually release precipitation, restarting the cycle once again. If it is helpful for you, you can draw pictures in your diagram as well.

The cycle diagram can be useful for scientific topics, such as biological processes, and also can apply to ideas and themes in literary works.

Cycle Diagrams

The Water Cycle

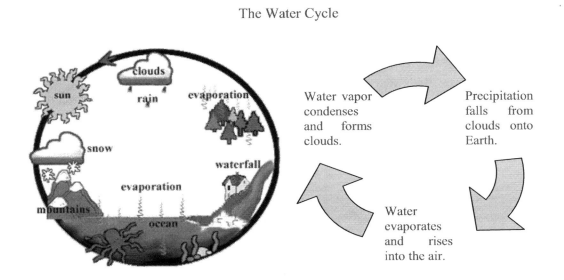

❖   **The Tree Design**

The tree format shows relationships between objects or ideas; it is often used to display familial relationships. My ancestral tree is shown on the following page. It shows a clear line of descent from my grandparents at the top of the tree to their grandchildren at the bottom. A tree can be used for other purposes as well, such as to show the division of a country in the aftermath of a major war or to help you keep track of characters in a novel. While versatile in its applications, you will generally find the tree best suited for science, language arts, and history courses.

The Tree Design

My Family Tree

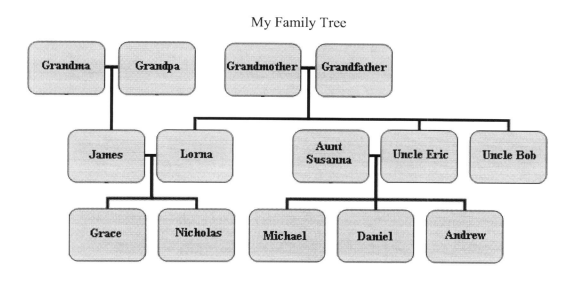

When deciding on how to format your notes, choose the method that is best for you. Be creative and adapt or alter these techniques as needed. For instance, you could turn the tree design on its side to better accommodate certain subject material. Remember that in general it is best to only deviate from the general note-taking format if you need to compare and contrast topics or if a more specific format will help you to understand the material better.

❖ **When You Have a Question or Fall Behind**

When you take notes, you need to get the correct information. If you are unsure of what you heard, or if you missed something your teacher said, don't just let it go. Your teacher will not accept incorrect information on your tests. This section will help you to keep your notes accurate and will teach you what you need to do if you miss something the teacher says.

First and foremost, always stay calm. Don't panic if you miss a sentence or if you don't understand something, even if all the other students seem to be understanding. If you let panic control your actions, you will end up missing more information and upsetting yourself unnecessarily. In your notes, leave a gap large enough to handle the information you missed or do not understand. Then, channel your aggravation into energy you can use to catch up with the teacher. Keep your mind relaxed and imagine a burst of energy entering your writing hand to help you catch up. Write as quickly as you can to get everything down. Only in such scenarios, in which you are either lost or confused, should you write everything and stop filtering the information for the important items. You need to get *everything* down because you cannot accurately filter if you are confused or have missed some information relevant to what your teacher is now saying. Also, put a question mark (?) in the margin nearby so that when you go over your notes later you will be alerted that this was a section that confused you. You will have time to look over and correct your notes at that time. Often, since you took good notes before the problematic information and then took extensive notes afterwards, you will be able to fill in what you missed.

There are several ways you can clarify problems you encountered while taking notes. Firstly, you can talk to your teacher about the issue. Immediately raise your hand for help if you fall off track during class. However, if you are not able to resolve the problem during class, let it go. Meet with your teacher after class when he or she has time to offer you an adequate explanation. In addition to your teacher, you can also go to another student for help. As we discussed before, other students make mistakes, and, especially if you were confused by a particular topic, they very well could have been, too. Only go to a reliable student you include or want to include in your network. In addition to going to another student, you also have the option of looking up the information in your textbook or looking it up online. Reading about the topic in the text should clarify the matter for you.

Often it is important to correct any problems you may have in class immediately. If, for instance, you cannot clearly see your teacher's visual presentation, raise your hand right away and let him know so that you do not fall behind. If a word comes up that you are unable to understand or spell, then it is generally best for you to write your best guess of the spelling for the word and then add *sp* in the margin nearest the word. When you get home, look the word up in the dictionary or in your textbook. It is important to know how to spell the words that come up in your notes. Even if they are not new key terms, just as you are using them in your notes you may one day need to use them in a written assignment on the same subject. Take the extra effort to learn to spell the particular word correctly. If your teacher keeps using a new word throughout class one day, you may decide to go ahead and ask him about it during class.

It is important for you to know that asking questions is a good thing. Do not feel afraid, embarrassed, or uncool asking a question. There are students out there with these perceptions wrongly imprinted in their young minds, and as a result they will miss out on countless learning opportunities throughout their lives. Interactive learning is a beautiful thing. Being able to formulate and ask a question, be answered, and understand that answer is a satisfying and maturing experience. When you have a question, be proud that you have a question, as doing so shows that you are a conscientious student who has the knowledge and brainpower necessary to take the subject matter into your own hands. As we discussed before, think over what you already know first. Then, using what you know, and what you don't, form a specific question to ask your teacher. Of course, you don't want to interrupt class constantly with your questions. If you are ever just a little confused or unsure of something you wrote, all you have to do is stick a question mark (?) in the adjacent margin. Your teacher may eventually answer the question on his or her own, another student may ask it, or you might figure it out yourself. After class, you can look up any information you need or ask a friend or the teacher for help.

Finally, if you miss a class or part of a class, make sure to get notes from someone else right away. If you know ahead of time that you won't be there, try making plans for someone else to cover for you. Tell a student you trust in academics that you are not going to be in class, and ask if you can copy his or her notes over at a later time. Since you have to depend on another student in this case, do your best to ensure that the student you choose is someone you can trust to take the class seriously. If you can't make arrangements until after the missed class time, then do all you can to get the notes *physically* in your hands as soon as possible. If you allow too much time to pass by, you may end up never getting the notes or not knowing which class you missed. Once you get the notes, photocopy them and give them back quickly and in the same condition you received them. You want to be able to borrow from this

> *Be careful when photocopying notes. Check the copied version to make sure none of the original information got cut off. Check each page and fill in wherever necessary.*

person again if necessary. In general, unless the notes are very short or you don't have a photocopier, don't bother hand-copying the notes. Photocopying the information will take up much less of your time so you will have more time to review and learn the new information.

❖ Writing Quickly and Efficiently

> *Most teachers speak at about 100 words per minute (wpm). Unfortunately, students typically write only at about 25 wpm. Using shorthand, the average person can increase their writing speed to about 100 wpm or more!*

Your teacher can most likely speak much more quickly than you can write. Ironically, your job is to write down what your teacher says. Of course, we have already discussed that you are only going to write down a limited amount of what your teacher says. Even so, your teacher can still get ahead of you in your notes. This section is loaded with the helpful tips that successful students use every day to get their notes down quickly and accurately.

To take notes quickly, you need to use shorthand and abbreviations and to leave out unnecessary words. Shorthand lets you reduce long or often-repeated words to just a few letters or a quick symbol. On the following page is a list of commonly used shorthand and symbols.

Common Shorthand

with; within; without	w/; w/in; w/o
and	&
because	b/c; bc
therefore	∴
is; equals; agrees; can; defined as	=
isn't; disagrees	≠
approximately	≈
plus; in addition; positive	+
minus; negative	-
money; dollars	$
less than; smaller	<
greater than; larger	>
increase; big	↑
decrease; little	↓
number	#
change	Δ
causes; leads/changes to	→
before	b4
multiplied by; times	X
female; girl; woman	♀
male; boy; man	♂
degree	°

You can abbreviate a long word or phrase into a smaller recognizable set of letters. When you find yourself frequently using a long word in your notes, come up with a logical abbreviation for it. Write the abbreviation and what it stands for in the margin; for example, if you were taking notes on short-term memory, you would write *STM = short-term memory* in the margin and then use that abbreviation throughout your notes. This way, you will be sure to understand the abbreviation when it comes time to review your notes. Listed on the following page are some common abbreviations.

Common Abbreviations

people → ppl
environment → env
government → gvt
point → pt
through → thru
especially → esp
et cetera → etc.
example → ex.
regarding → re:
in other words; that is → i.e.
for example; such as → e.g.

_____ → _____

_____ → _____

_____ → _____

_____ → _____

Always have in mind that the purpose of your notes is for you to be able to use them at some later point to review what you learned in class.

Memorize the symbols and their meanings from the common shorthand list. The symbols cover words that you will need to write often throughout your notes. If you come across another word you use frequently, you can shorthand it by creating your own symbol or abbreviation for it and defining it in the margin. Also, be on the lookout for any other symbols you may find useful in your note-taking. You can add your ideas to either of the appropriate lists above.

Just as you abbreviate words, you should also abbreviate your sentences. This

means you should get rid of any extra words, such as *the* and *a*. Don't use complete sentences in your notes; instead use only phrases and groups of words to get the needed point across. If you are doing it right, your notes should read like a caveman's script in a movie—lacking the verb *to be* and any definite or indefinite articles. Your notes need to be succinct and still get the point across.

Putting these ideas together, if your biology teacher said "The adhesive forces allow the water molecules to stick to and climb up walls," you would simply jot down *adhesive force lets water molecs stick to & climb ↑ wall*.

Keep in mind that time is always a factor in your note-taking. If you ever have a break or slow time in class, make use of that. Read over your notes to make sure they are understandable; cross your *t*'s and dot your *i*'s. Fill in any gaps you left to come back to later. See the review box below for a summary of how to take notes.

That was a lot of information! Let's review the key strategies for efficient note-taking:

- *Write legibly and only on one side of each page.*
- *The general format of note-taking is applicable in almost every situation. Leave the margins empty, and create a bullet for each main category. List beneath the bullet all information that falls into that category, marking each new line with a dash. Any specific detail, side point, or example gets an indented dash.*
- *Write 'CONT:' before switching to a category you already bulleted and took notes on. Underline key words; place an asterisk before or a box around important information; write 'MEM' in the margin next to information you need to memorize.*
- *To compare and contrast, you may want to set up your notes as a T-chart or Venn diagram. T-charts are best for showing direct contrasts, while Venn diagrams highlight overlap between topics.*
- *When applicable, you can also take notes in one of the following styles: the pyramid method, cycle diagram, or tree design.*
- *If you fall way off track while taking notes, don't panic. Leave an appropriately sized space in your notes so that you can fill in the missing information later, and put a question mark in the margin. Then, focus all of your energy on writing everything else your teacher says relating to the topic of confusion.*
- *If you are unsure as to how to spell a particular word, mark it in the margin with 'sp,' and find out its correct spelling as soon as possible.*
- *If you need to clarify a section of your notes after class, put a question mark in the adjacent margin.*
- *Write your notes using shorthand and symbols, abbreviations, and condensed sentences.*

SUMMARY: IN THE CLASSROOM

- Show everyone what a serious student you are. Always come to class on time and be prepared.

- Sit up front and participate in class discussions.

- Set participation goals, and plan what you want to say before coming to class.

- To keep on track, always look at the face of the individual speaking. Doing so keeps you alert and shows others that you are paying attention.

- When you ask a question, summarize relevant background information and be specific.

- Boredom happens. If you get distracted, gently pull your mind back to the classroom. You can jot down what you were thinking about on your to-do list if you want to consider the matter more later.

- Your teacher is also a person, and he or she is not always perfect or correct. Remember to *treat others as you would like to be treated.*

- Try to figure out what your teacher considers to be important regarding the course material, as these topics will certainly be on your test.

- Teachers sometimes make extra help available. Go if you have specific questions you need the teacher to answer. If your teacher offers to read over rough drafts of written assignments, take advantage of the opportunity.

- Be careful not to offend your teacher. Keep on good communicative terms with him or her.

- Read over the notes review box on page 83.

5. At Home

••

Your teachers expect you to do work both in and out of class. In addition to completing your assignments in a timely manner, you also need to accomplish your own personal academic tasks. This section explains how to handle both assigned and unassigned projects. We will go over how you should review your notes, analyze readings, and do your homework.

Reviewing Your Notes

Almost every day, you will leave school with new notes, in-class assignments, and handouts. You should aim to review this material at home on a daily basis. It is generally best to review new material for a specific course before doing the homework for that class. In that way, you will be able to test and reinforce your new knowledge while working on the homework. As you saw in **Scheduling**, it is a good idea to list *reviewing your notes* in your homework planner and to make it a part of your schedule. In Nick's schedule for Spanish class on page 54, he included two aspects of reviewing his notes. One was listing all of the new vocabulary words from that day's lesson, and the other was spending time reviewing the new words. While in general neither Nick nor you need to spend time rewriting notes, in this instance it was beneficial for him in that doing so allowed him to see the new words in a clear and compact format rather than in the interspersed way in which they were originally written in his notes. In this section we will discuss how to organize your notes and other course materials at home and how to go about reviewing the material.

As you know, your study spot will be the home for all academic materials that you do not physically need to have with you at school. In your study spot, there will be several large binders containing dividers marked for each one of your courses. Any time you complete a full page of notes for a particular course, add those notes in the proper order to the appropriate section of the binder. In the *History* division, for instance, the first page of the section will be the notes from your very first class and the last page will be the most recently completed full page of history notes. As discussed previously, any partially completed page will be used to continue the next day's notes. If you ever accidentally do not finish a complete page before going on to a new page of notes, simply draw a diagonal line across the empty space before adding it to your large binder. That way, when you review later you will know that you went on to a new sheet and are not missing anything. Any handouts, assignments, or old tests should be added to this section of your binder as well. Usually, it is best to hole punch them and include them in chronological order interspersed throughout your notes. The majority of your notes and handouts will be at home in your study spot. Even if you cannot leave your new notes home because you still need them at school, bring them home just for the day so that you can review and highlight them.

> *My father and his best friend used to come home from high school every day and study hard in case they would have a pop quiz the next day. Sometimes, they did. It happened to them, it happened to me, and it will happen to you. It pays to be prepared!*

As you saw with the general note-taking format, when you review your notes, you will basically be reading through a long list of information. However, remember that there is a common theme tying the facts together—the big picture. Think about it this way. If you were to look at a painting of a farm, you would notice the details of the picture: the farmhouse, farmer, crops, fences, and animals. The artist uses all of these details to create what you see as a picture of a farm, the big picture. You can apply this concept to your notes. Your teacher gave you many little facts and details. Look at them and ask yourself, what is he or she *drawing* for me? What does this information mean when you put it all together, and what is its significance? When you review your notes, do it with the mindset of trying to see the big picture. This will help you to understand the purpose of the smaller details and to better remember the information.

Furthermore, your notes for a class should show an element of continuity. If you do not see a connection between your new notes and previous ones, or if you do not understand your new notes, you need to address the problem. It is essential that you put in the required time and effort to understand every piece of information in your notes. Your notes, after all, include only that information you selected as important. Look up the information you need in your textbook. If that is not sufficient, ask a friend or the teacher for help. So you don't forget, write in your homework planner what you need to ask your teacher. When you are able to approach your teacher for help, you can let him or her know that you tried looking up the information on your own first.

You are now going to learn a new system for reviewing your notes. In this system, you will read your newest notes on a daily basis, and you will frequently review your older notes to keep the material fresh in your mind.

Typically, when you come home from school, you will have new notes and assignments for each class. Try to first review your notes for a particular class and then do the related assignments. In that way, you will be able to immediately put your new knowledge to use. Once you are completely done reviewing your notes and doing your assignments for a particular class, move on to a different class.

In order to use this system, read the notes you took that day in full. If there are any gaps or points of confusion, fill them in or correct them. Make sure you understand everything in these new notes. Remember to thoroughly review any hand-outs or other new materials you received that day in addition to your notes. You often will need to make a few tweaks to the content, removing some repetitive or wrong information or adding further explanatory information. *After* you have fully reviewed your latest notes and hand-outs for a class, take out a highlighter and highlight points in the material that you want to focus on learning, such as items that you have to memorize, that you think you may have trouble remembering, or that seem very important. The following day, when you review your newest notes for the day, you will also review the highlighted information from the previous days. In general, I recommend reading all of your previously highlighted information in chronological order before studying the new notes for the day, so as to reinforce the continuity of the material.

As the school days continue on, you will have more and more to study during each note review session. You will also become more and more familiar with much of the highlighted information, as you will be reviewing it on a daily basis. When you decide you know a specific highlighted piece of text so well that you no longer need to review it on a daily basis, put a large check mark by it in the adjacent margin. That way, when reviewing highlights, you will know you do not need to review that one when you get to it.

Do not feel as though you *have to* highlight something on every piece of paper. Often, class handouts and worksheets contain primarily information that you already have in your notes. If you feel like the information on a handout is out of the scope of the course material, you can always clarify with your teacher by asking if you will be responsible for specific information on the handout. If your teacher says that a particular handout is relevant test material, or if it appears that your teacher himself created the handout (rather than it being mass-produced by a distant manufacturer), consider it of special importance.

Your mind is like a sponge; frequently review your notes and over time you will commit to memory and better understand the information. Only review that material that will be on your next exam. If the exam is not a cumulative one, you will not need to study all of the material you have in your binder. Overall, aim for your notes review session for a particular class to take under half an hour. Also, don't dwell over each piece of information. Simply read it so that it makes sense to you, and then go on. Your job during review time is not to memorize, it is simply to review and to understand. Your mind creates its own memory of the information through your understanding of it.

It is optimal to review your notes for each class every day. If you ever fall behind in reviewing your notes, make a concerted effort to catch up. Although the weekend offers time to make up for missed work, it is best not to put work off because other demands may be made on your time.

This is an effective and simple method of learning. It will provide you with continuity and will reinforce old ideas in your head before you look over the new information. Learning information is easier the second, third, fourth, or fifth time around. This system ensures you understand your course material well. If you come across something you do not understand, there is time to ask your teacher for help well before any test. Since you will work on a little new learning and memorization every day, you will not have to cram before tests for unreasonable amounts of time, and you will have an understanding and comfort with the course material during class. This is all made possible through your daily review. Do not allow yourself to skip review time; it is key to your academic success.

Students often wonder if they should rewrite their notes during their review sessions. Actually, it depends. For example, if you think your notes look messy and disorganized, that alone does not mean you should rewrite them. If your notes are messy, but you are easily able to read and study from them, then you don't need to rewrite them. However, if you would be able to study more quickly and efficiently with more neatly written notes, then it is worth your while to rewrite them. You only want to spend your valuable time doing something if you know that it is going to benefit you in the long run. Sometimes, I like to type up my notes because then, when I am looking for a certain section in my notes, I can simply type a keyword or phrase into the search box and quickly find the section of my notes for which I am looking. Furthermore, rewriting notes can help you to further familiarize yourself with the content. It also enables you to write your notes in a format more appropriate to the content they contain. You may wish to take information from your notes comparing democracy and communism, for instance, and place them in a T-chart. You might be able to understand and remember your history class notes better in the format of a detailed timeline. For a language course, you can do as Nick did and place your new vocabulary words in an ongoing list you keep throughout the course. The take-home point is that you should only spend time rewriting your notes if you feel that it will truly help you to better understand, remember, and apply the information. Remember, when you do rewrite your notes, only highlight those items that continue to require further study or memorization.

> My father once took a course on human rights. Often, he would learn some about the contributions of one thinker or leader, such as Confucius, Adam Smith, or one of the Thomases (Aquinas, Hobbes, and Jefferson), and then several classes later the discussion would return to that individual again. As time went on, my father began to have a hard time remembering and contrasting who said what. Therefore, he rewrote his notes according to philosopher; he would bullet each individual's name and then write the relevant beliefs and ideals of that individual. He also wrote a brief timeline for the American and French Revolutions, which were pivotal in the subject's history. This helped my father to understand and more easily access his notes. When an in-class open-notebook test rolled around asking about the significance of these wars and philosophers, my father was able to quickly and fully answer the questions. Meanwhile, his classmates had to spend much of their precious test time flipping through pages of notes and searching for the necessary names and ideas.

Reading the Text

It may seem as if there is nothing special to know about how to read a textbook. You pick it up and read, right? Actually, that is not the most efficient approach. People often end up reading through material without gaining any substantial new knowledge from it. Reading a textbook, or any class-related material, is a crucial part of learning and requires your active involvement in the process. In this section you will learn what to do to get through your reading assignments quickly and with maximal comprehension. We will also analyze the pros and cons of supplementary readings.

❖ **Long-term Reading Assignments**

Teachers often assign reading for homework. Clearly, being the success-minded student you are, you will want to complete any assigned and to do a good job. The only question for you will be how to handle it.

For readings that will take several hours, plan short intermittent breaks every hour or so. If you find during your hour that you are working well and on a role, *in the zone* as they say, then take advantage of it and keep going strong without stopping. If you do not get in the zone, no worries; focus on working solid for that hour of reading and look forward to your break that is soon to come. During your break, do something different to change the pace. Walk around, do a quick and easy homework assignment, fold your laundry, anything that will be a break from your reading. Then you can get back to your next hour of reading with a fresh mind.

When you are assigned a long term reading project, such as a text that will take several days or more to complete, immediately plan how you will break the reading up over time. Find the total number of pages you are going to read, and divide that number by the number of nights you have left until you  need to have the reading assignment complete. Your answer, called the quotient, is the minimum number of pages you should be reading daily. Make sure not to miss days because doing so will double your work for the next day, and your workload may quickly become overwhelming. Also, in order to keep the readings as manageable as possible, I like to leave in a few buffer days so that I usually end up finishing the assignment a couple days ahead of time. To add in buffer time, you can either add five pages or so to your daily reading requirement, or you can recalculate as follows: take the total number of pages you have to read and divide it by two or three less than the number of reading days you have remaining. This way you will have a couple of free days that will give you time to catch up if you fall behind your reading schedule. After you have done the calculations, fill in your homework planner on the appropriate days with these small reading assignments.

❖ **Increasing Your Reading Speed**

When you read, you want to read efficiently, quickly, and with comprehension. To achieve this, try practicing with some light reading material. Pick out a few items that you like to read for fun, such as the daily newspaper, your favorite magazine, or a novel you enjoy. When you have the chance, sit down and read one of these, reading as quickly as you can while maintaining comprehension. This will be a little uncomfortable for you, but it will train your mind to read at a faster pace. Avoid stopping and going back to reread sentences, as doing so will slow you down unnecessarily.

> *Wow, that's fast! On July 7th, 1999, Hicham El Guerrouj of Morocco set the world record for the men's one mile race. He clocked in at 3 minutes and 43.13 seconds while racing in Rome.*

Visualization has been shown to improve reading speed. In addition to practicing the above, try the following. As you read, imagine yourself walking quickly. Hear the thud as your sneaker hits the pavement with each stride. Then, match your strides to your reading rate. Imagine yourself moving faster and faster to get yourself reading faster and faster.

Continue to practice these methods whenever you pick up any light reading material. As you progress, you will start to feel more comfortable reading at a faster pace, which will come in handy when you have a large reading assignment.

❖ **Improving Comprehension**

Whenever you read, whether it be for leisure or for school, it is smart to have a good dictionary by your side. That way you can look up any new or ambiguous words right away. Furthermore, the presence of the dictionary alone may stimulate you to look up words you may have otherwise skipped over.

You want to understand everything your reading assignment says. If you come across some information that does not make sense to you, grab a piece of paper and write down the page number and section of the problematic information along with your specific question. Later, try to understand the confusing material. Actively reading and questioning the material in this way will take your understanding and retention of the information to a whole new level.

It is often helpful with difficult assignments to be able to write on the assignment itself, highlighting and summarizing information directly on the document. This is generally most beneficial for assignments that require a degree of interpretation. In this way, you will be able to decipher the meaning of the text as you go, writing small summaries in the margin of the text. If you are given reading material that you would like to write on but that you are not allowed to mark, photocopy it and write on the copy. This has the added benefit of allowing you to carry the copied pages around with you instead of the entire book from which they came. While reading, have a highlighter and a pen handy. Whenever you come across a word, phrase, sentence or paragraph that is especially helpful toward your understanding of the piece, highlight it. Then, use your pen to write in the adjacent margin a brief generalization of what you highlighted. For example, if you were reading *Romeo and Juliet* and you came across a particularly significant section, you would highlight the key phrases and then summarize them in the margin. The summary need not be lengthy, a simple *Tybalt stabs Mercutio* will suffice. In this way, you will be actively involved in understanding and interpreting the meaning of the piece. Your highlighted sections are insightful phrases that come directly from the text, and the few words you write in the margins allow you to easily see what happened in the piece without having to reread or figure out the entire piece again. This greatly simplifies things when you come back to the document for an assignment, class discussion ideas, or test preparation.

> *If you don't have easy access to a photocopy machine, try finding a reliable place that has them, such as your school library, a teacher's office, the local public library, or a copy or office supply store. Many home scanning devices can make copies if you have only a few pages.*

❖ Improving Retention: Outlines

The above method is best used to improve reading comprehension. For many assignments, however, you will not need to focus on interpreting the information but rather on remembering it. To vastly improve your retention, you will use an outline—an organized paper detailing all significant topics in your reading. Creating an outline forces you to be more involved with the text and provides you with a condensed version of all of the information you need to know from the reading. Furthermore, in **Test Time**, you will learn how a few additional steps can transform your outline into a comprehensive test study guide. Since your outline will only be a few pages, it will be easy to carry around with you and study wherever you go.

All items from your reading that are important enough for you to be tested on belong on your outline. Whenever you do an assigned reading for class, you will make an outline containing any significant points. You should either type your outline or write it in pen so that it will not smudge. Many students find it easier to type their outlines as it enables them to add new information while maintaining order.

When you have completed your outline, you will bring it with you to class. This is where the colored pens and highlighters that we discussed in **Tools for School** will come in use. In class, you can highlight anything your teacher points out as especially important, and you can write any extra notes directly onto your outline under the correct Roman numeral headings, soon to be discussed. The reason you need different colored pens in class is so that you can easily discern between what you wrote on your original outline (if you wrote it in pen) and what you later added in class. When handwriting my original outline, I use black pen and then later add notes with a blue pen or red pen in class. As with your notes, try to only write on one side of the page. On the back, you can list any questions or points of confusion you have. Your colored pens will often come into use in other situations in the classroom as well. For instance, if your teacher tries to depict a progression of events using only one diagram, you can use a different color to show each step. Then, write on the side of the diagram *blue=1ˢᵗ, red=2ⁿᵈ,* and so on.

The format of your outline is simple and is optimal for easy review and comprehension. At the top of the page, write your name, the date, the chapter number and title, and the initial page number you are outlining. Leave a space and then write Roman numeral one (I.) in the margin. Directly to the right of the number, write the topic for that

In general, it is good practice to put your name and the day's date on all of your documents.

section. If the chapter you are reading is divided into subtopics, as many textbooks are, you can use each subheading as a cue for the next Roman numeral and topic on your outline. Try to include page numbers with your Roman numeral headings so that you will easily be able to refer back to the text if needed.

On the next line, just to the right of the margin, write the letter *A*. You do not want to skip lines on your outline as you want the information to be compact and easy to carry around. Underneath the Roman numeral, you will list the relevant information, starting with point *A*. Continue writing each important fact that falls into that topic, following with *B, C, D*, and so on. You will at times run into significant details pertaining specifically to one of your lettered points. In such cases, indent directly beneath that letter and note it using a lower case Roman numeral (i.). If you find an important point that applies to that lower case Roman numeral, then you can indent beneath it and write a lower case letter (a.). For a detail you need to add below a lower case letter, simply use the Arabic numerals *1, 2, 3*, and so on.

Write your outline in words you can understand, and use abbreviated language to cut down on time and space. See Nick's example on the following page for an application of the above. It may seem like a lot of information right now, but you will find that if you are diligent with this, in no time you are going to adapt. Refer back here as often as necessary. You may want to mark this page with a label or fold down the page corner for easy reference.

Nick's Biology Outline

Nicholas Charles
December 9, 2009
Chapter 4, *Biological Growth and Development*, p. 81

I.   Embryonic development (p184)
    A. Embryonic cells undergo mitosis and differentiation
          i. Mitosis is the cell division process
               a. Consists of prophase, metaphase, anaphase, telophase, & cytokinesis
          ii. Differentiation makes them specialized in structure & function
    B. Morphogenesis = development of body shape & organization
          i. Occurs during ontogeny
               a. Ontogeny = embryonic development of organism
II.   Different types of cells in an organism have the same DNA (p193)
    A. Cells differ in structure & function b/c express different portions of common genome
          i. Not because they contain different genes
    B. Differentiated cells from mature plants are often totipotent
          i. Totipotent: capable of generating complete new plant
               a. Toti = all; potent = powerful
    C. Differentiated animal cell nucleus sometimes = new animal if transplanted → enucleated egg cell
          i. Enucleated = the nucleus has been removed

In case you don't know all the Roman numerals, they are listed in both upper and lower case along with their corresponding Arabic equivalents on the following page. If you have difficulty with them, you can use the Arabic numerals in their place (1, 2, 3…). It is best to use Roman numerals if you can, as you will be less likely to confuse Roman numerals with the information on your outline, and Roman numerals will also allow you a greater degree of organization in your writing than will Arabic numerals.

Need to brush up on your Roman numerals? No problem! Roman numerals are actually pretty simple as long as you know that:
- *'I' has a value of one, 'V' = five, 'X' = ten*
- *To write a number, you must combine the numerals to equate to that value. If the single value digits are placed before a 'V' or 'X,' they are subtracted from it; if they are placed afterwards, they are added.*
  - *For example, 'IX' is 9, but 'XI' is 11.*
- *You can use a maximum of three single digits (I) in a row before switching to the next numeral value and using subtraction.*
  - *For example, 8 is* VIII, *but 9 is* IX.

Roman and Arabic Numerals

1	2	3	4	5	6	7	8	9	10	11	12	13	14	15
I	II	III	IV	V	VI	VII	VIII	IX	X	XI	XII	XIII	XIV	XV
i	ii	iii	iv	v	vi	vii	viii	ix	x	xi	xii	xiii	xiv	xv

When working on a reading assignment, there are several ways to tell if the information you are reading is of importance. One major way the authors of a textbook communicate importance is by **bolding**, *italicizing*, or underlining an item. They will also emphasize certain items by showing pictures, charts, or diagrams to help you understand. Make sure you can understand these depictions and what they mean. Often, diagram captions do an excellent job of explaining tough subjects and longwinded passages.

The topics the authors mention in the introduction to a chapter are also useful. Some textbooks list the most important topics at the beginning of the chapter. From this list, you will know right away what the major headings of your outline should include. Also, at the end of each chapter, many authors put a concluding section or a bulleted list summarizing the whole chapter. These review the *main points* of the chapter and are concepts with which you need to be familiar. As tempting as it may be, do not skip the chapter and just read the summary. Summary boxes leave out *major details* and ideas that you need to know for your outline, class exams, and personal understanding.

Your outline is the most useful piece of study material you have. Review it on a daily basis, preferably along with your daily notes review sessions. Have your outline out while reviewing notes and working on class assignments, both so you can refer to it and so you can add on any relevant information. Ultimately, you want to have all of the information you need to know for the next test on one outline or on one set of outlines—assuming the test is on multiple reading assignments—that you clip together; more on that in **Test Time**.

I often like to photocopy my outlines so that I can carry them around with me without worrying about if the original gets lost or dirty. Read over your outlines whenever you have some extra review time. You can look over your outline before your teacher starts class, on the bus, at lunch, etc. By putting to use your small bits of free time in this way, you will constantly be confirming in your mind the specific information that you need to know to do well in class. Thanks to this regular review and in-depth understanding of the material, when it comes time for a test, pop quiz, or graded assignment, you will know your stuff!

❖ **Reading a Math Textbook**

Math tends to be different than other subjects in that the majority of its work requires neither memorization nor interpretation, but application. In math, you need to have an understanding of the concepts and to be able to apply them to various new problems. This can be difficult to teach, and many math textbooks have trouble getting the know-how across to student readers.

If you need to read a math textbook, turn to the appropriate section in the book and start to read. As you go, decide if you are able to understand the odd little symbols and abbreviations that math textbooks typically use. If not, look for a key to the symbols in the very back or front of the book. If there is not one, look through the preceding lessons. They will most likely define any unclear words or symbols that appear in the current lesson. Also, the definitions of any math-related terms you do not know can be found in the glossary or index at the back of the book or in most good dictionaries. Once you have an understanding of the meaning of the mathematical terms and symbols, you can go on reading the text.

With math, it is especially important to understand each sentence you read before going on to the next, as the concepts tend to build on one another. The sample problems your book offers will often do much better to teach you than the words describing them, so make sure to analyze the problems closely. Understand each step of the problem before you move on to the next step. Once you think you have the hang of it, try to do one of the sample problems on your own without looking at the way the book did it first. When trying to answer a sample problem, write your work out on paper so that you can make deliberate choices and record your thoughts on how to solve the problem. This way, if you get stuck, you will be able to compare your ideas to the book's solution and see at what step you went wrong. After using this method to read a section of your math textbook, you will be ready to do the problems presented in that lesson. If while reading you came across any key concepts or helpful tips, make sure to write them down. Create a short outline including the useful items or add the information to your math notes.

❖ Supplementary Readings

Supplementary readings are books selected by you to use in addition to your normal classroom texts. You do not necessarily need these. If you find, however, that a certain class is exceedingly difficult, or that your textbook is too advanced or verbose for you to understand in a reasonable amount of time, you should consider getting some supplementary texts. You can ask your teacher if there are any supplementary books he recommends on the subject, or you can do your own browsing and research. Bookstores and libraries carry many books that focus on helping high school students understand a multitude of subjects, including Biology, Algebra, U.S. History, and Chemistry. The companies that make these student guides write them in readable language and try hard to teach you everything your textbook is supposed to. They can be very helpful.

If you decide to get one or a few supplementary readings for a class, check your school or local public libraries first. That way, you can check them out for free before you buy them. Also, when shopping for a supplementary textbook, bring your class syllabus along with you and compare it with the table of contents of the supplementary text. You want to find a text that covers the material you are expected to know. You generally will not need more than one extra book for a class because you won't have time to be reading multiple books for each class. If you are planning on taking a standardized test, such as the SAT II, for a particular course, it will be particularly beneficial for you to purchase a supplementary text specifically geared toward that subject test. This will provide you with a second text for content explanation and with test-specific practice problems and advice.

> *There are many book companies that make high school subject guides, including Kaplan, Barron's, Cliffs Notes, SparkNotes, and even a "For Dummies" series. Check book reviews on www.amazon.com to select the book most appropriate for you. Amazon also often allows you to view pages of the prospective text, including the Table of Contents and the back cover information. If that option is available, read through some of the pages of the text, and decide if you like the way the material is presented.*

Doing Your Homework

It is vital to your success that you do all your homework. To do your homework, you need to know what the assignments are and how to complete them. You also need to know how to handle large projects and make your schedule accordingly. In this section, we will discuss these items along with how to reach maximum efficiency while working on your homework.

In **Scheduling**, we briefly discussed the uses of your homework planner. In your planner, you will write down all of your academic assignments and commitments. By the end of each class, you should have recorded that class' long- and short-term assignments into your planner for the day. For instance, if your first class of the day was Spanish, then by the end of Spanish class you would have written in your homework planner 'Spanish—' and after the dash you would write any new assignments. When you have multiple assignments, write them down in list format so that you can check them off as you complete each individual assignment. For example, you would write:

Spanish— Do green packet

—Do worksheet *El/La*

Keep in mind that reading counts as an assignment. Also, if you have absolutely nothing you need to do for a class then simply write the subject and *none* so that you will not be confused later as to if you simply had no homework or if you forgot to record the assignment. Whenever you complete an assignment, check off the line on which that assignment was written.

√Spanish— Do green packet

√   —Do worksheet *El/La*

At the end of the day you should have one continuous column of check marks.

Long-term assignments require an extra step of work, but in general they are no more difficult than short-term assignments. As you probably have noticed by now,  everything becomes much simpler once you break it down. Long-term assignments are no exception. You need to break down any large, long-term assignments into smaller, more manageable short-term projects that you can do over time. The first day you are assigned a massive long-term project, your homework is to set aside time that day to break the project down and plan it out.

To begin with, take a look at the project requirements. If your teacher did not give you a list of requirements, make your own list. A research paper, for example, would require tasks such as creating a thesis, doing research at the library, and writing and editing the first draft. For each component, establish a due date for yourself. It would be wise to have your rough draft finished early so that you have time to review it and to have the teacher or somebody else go over it as well before handing it in. To have your rough draft ready by a certain date, set appropriate deadlines for completing all other portions of the paper beforehand. If you are planning a five page paper, you may decide to be up to page four at least three days before you plan to have a complete rough draft to show your teacher. After completing this process, go through your homework planner and add your project timetable and deadlines to the appropriate days. Write these commitments at the very top of the sections for each day, and when that day eventually arrives, add your new assignments below as you normally would. As you complete each part of the process, remember to look ahead in your planner so that you are aware of what step follows. You may also want to add these self-made deadlines to your large wall calendar to ensure that you do not lose track of them.

In addition to your assignments, you should also include assigned project deadlines, future commitments, and test dates in your planner. Remember to mark these dates on your wall calendar as well. In your planner, write these items on the top portion of the corresponding days. This way, when flipping through your homework planner you will see what you have coming up. For instance, if you have a biology test next Thursday, then go ahead and write at the top of your block for next Thursday *Biology Test*. If your daily planner is divided with a different section for each course, then write *Biology Test* at the top of the biology section. You will still have room to add new commitments underneath the test listing, and you will be able to use your planner to avoid scheduling conflicts.

One key for doing your homework efficiently is to focus on fulfilling your maximum work potential. Many students do their schoolwork without noticing the pace at which they are completing it. However, if you keep track of your time, you can greatly increase your efficiency—you have done it before. For instance, do you remember that time when you were only partway through a test and your teacher announced that there were only two minutes left? Suddenly, you were working at three times the rate you were working before. Or, what about the time your mom called while you were doing your homework and told you she would be picking you up in five minutes for a rescheduled doctor's appointment, didn't you rush to finish those last few problems so you would be done before she picked you up? In both instances, you were able to pick up the pace on demand without sacrifice much in terms of quality. *You improved your efficiency.*

Consciously press yourself to work more quickly. Before you begin an assignment, set a time by which you think you can have it completed, and then get to work trying to beat the deadline. Another option is to make a commitment to yourself to work solid, such as deciding that you will not get up from the table until you have completed at least ten pages of your history reading assignment. There is no reason to waste your time working slowly when you can do just as well working at a faster pace. As you work quickly, keep in mind that soon you will be taking your periodic break to refresh your mind and relax some.

If at times you feel overwhelmed by your academic workload, don't worry. It happens to everyone. Especially if you are tired, you will be prone to distractions and may skimp on work quality. As we discussed in **The Smart Attitude**, so much of what successful students do depends on maintaining a confident, success-oriented attitude. Recognize that you hold your own future in the palm of your hands. Putting in the extra effort now will have exponentially greater results in the future.

SUMMARY: AT HOME

- Review your new class material every day. Complete your review before moving on to the related assignments.

- During your review, highlight sections of your notes that you need to study further.

- If you get confused, take action; look up your question in your textbook or go to the teacher.

- Break down long reading assignments. For those that will take several days or more to complete, find the total number of pages you have to read and divide it by the number of nights you have until the due date. This is the minimum number of pages you should be reading daily.

- Supplementary readings may help you to understand information that is not explained well in your textbook or with which you are having difficulty.

- Practice reading quickly on fun and interesting reading material. Picture the jogger in your mind to help speed up your reading. It works!

- To improve comprehension, highlight useful information and summarize it in the margins.

- Write your outline using upper and lower case Roman numerals (I, i, II, ii) and letters (A, a, B, b) as well as Arabic numbers (1, 2, 3). Write your outline in words you can understand, and use abbreviated language.

- Important information is often **bolded**, *italicized*, or underlined in reading assignments. It is also often depicted in diagrams and included in chapter summaries.

- When reading a math textbook, make sure you understand new concepts by following through and practicing sample problems.

- In your homework planner, write the assignments for each class as you go through your school day.

- When assigned a long-term project, immediately break it down into manageable pieces, and set deadlines for each piece. Include these in your homework planner.

- Fulfill your maximum potential by consciously putting pressure on yourself to work as quickly and efficiently as you can.

6. Test Time

Your test scores generally make up a good portion of your overall grade. To succeed in school, you need to do well on your tests. A test is meant to evaluate your knowledge and understanding of a subject. Everything we have discussed up to now will help you in your familiarity with and comprehension of the course material. In this section, you will learn the specific strategies that will bring you results on your tests, including a host of top memorization techniques. You will learn how to decipher tricky test questions, deal with different forms of questions, and answer questions to which you do not even know the answer. We will also discuss what to do with your test when you get it back so that you can keep your grades at their best. Finally, I will teach you some great relaxation techniques to help you through stressful times, including when you are studying for or taking your exam. As I explained in the very first chapter, your mindset is key and is the foundation for your success. You want to stay calm, stress-free, and focused on the test material.

Test Preparation

There are several key aspects to preparing well for any test. Basically, these aspects are covered by knowing the *who, what, where, when* and *how* of successful test preparation. In this section, we will respond to each of these topics, and we will also go into all other items of importance regarding your test preparation. This section includes a detailed description of study methods, memorization techniques, and last minute preparation tips.

❖ **When**

You have been reading and reviewing your notes every day. If there was something that was particularly difficult for you to remember or that took memorization, then you highlighted it. You have been looking over these highlights along with your outline and new notes in your daily reviews.

As usual, we broach test preparation by breaking it down and planning ahead. Mark the test date in your homework planner and wall calendar. Consider how much time you have between then and now. Divide the test material for which you are responsible in a logical way so that you can study pieces of it at a time. Usually, such material divides most easily by either general topics or textbook chapters. Plan to cover about an equal amount of time's worth of material every day until the test. Do not include the day before the test, though. This day must be reserved for a final review of all information. Depending how much material will be covered, you may want to leave two days before the test free for a full review of all you have studied.

Start your studying as soon as possible so that you will have ample time to study. If your teacher lets you know about a test early, he is trying to give you a head start. Take that time and put it to use. You need to study all necessary content piece by piece before the test. By starting early, you will have time to find out the answer to any questions that may arise while you are studying, and you will give yourself more time to get comfortable with the exam material. Write down in your homework planner for each day what studying you should be covering that day. Once you have studied something, you should have a solid knowledge and understanding of it so that you can move on to the next piece of your studying without having to return, except for a quick review of it on the following days. We will shortly discuss the route by which you will attain this solid understanding. Also, keep in mind that this studying is to be done in addition to your usual review of your notes and outlines. You do not want to fall behind in class while studying for your test. Furthermore, do not allow your studying schedule to get pushed off to the day before the test. That should be as relaxing a day as it can be, a day in which you simply look over material you already know.

Many people do not recognize it until they are much older, but the time of day really affects your ability to work. Almost everyone functions better at certain times of the day as opposed to others. It varies by individual. Some students work best in the afternoon, evening, or even late at night. Others are best able to concentrate after getting their excess energy out through exercise, no matter what the time of day. Of course, there are also those who are too fatigued to study after working out. Identify the time of day during which your mind is most sharp, when you feel calm and ready to study and work hard. This is the time during which you should work on your most difficult assignments and the time during which you should do the majority of your test preparation. You want the information you study to really stick with you.

It is best to study for the subject you are going to be tested on while in the frame of mind for that subject. So, if you are studying for history, go ahead and do your daily history notes review and homework for that day. Then, while your mind is still in history mode, move on to studying for your history test. Each subject takes its own unique frame of mind and thought process. You will find studying for math different than studying for biology, and studying biology different than studying for Spanish.

❖ **What to Expect**

Make sure you clearly understand on what information your teacher plans to test you. If you are not totally clear on this, go ahead and politely ask. If he or she goes by the book, ask which chapters and sections will be covered on the test. If he or she goes according to topic, make a list of prospective topics and ask about its accuracy to ensure you have everything on the list. Know whether the exam is cumulative or not. A cumulative exam will include all information that you learned in the class up to that point, while a noncumulative exam will only include what you have learned since the last test. Furthermore, some teachers base their exams on all the material they give out, including handouts, reading assignments, notes, etc., while other teachers only require you to know and understand the classroom lecture notes. It is important that you know where your teacher falls on this spectrum, otherwise you will end up either over- or under-studying for your exam. Over-studying can take up valuable study and work time that you need for your other courses.

On the following pages are four questions that you can answer to help you better predict and prepare for your exam. Provide specific responses to these questions before every exam. Below each question is information that will help you to give a more accurate answer, and further explanation is provided following the question set. Consider your teacher's ideology and personality when you respond. You can answer the questions in this book, make photocopies of these pages and write on those, or set up a notebook page in a similar manner. Physically writing your answers down will help you to get the most out of this exercise.

The 4 Keys to Predicting the Test

1. What source/s did your teacher rely on most to teach you the information for this particular test?

If your teacher mentioned a particular source on which he focused for material, you have your answer. If not, think about what source you learned most from; this is probably also where your teacher will look for information in order to make up your test.

_____
_____
_____
_____
_____
_____
_____
_____

2. From where did your teacher draw the questions for your homework and other assignments?

Questions similar to or the same as those your teacher assigned are very likely to show up on your test. Looking at the sources from where your teacher got the original questions will tell you about his or her focus and style of testing. Remember also to look in your notes for questions your teacher brought up during class.

_____
_____
_____
_____
_____
_____
_____
_____

3. To what extent does your teacher expect you to know the course material?

This can be a tough question. Teachers vary in their opinions as to what they think students should be responsible for in a course. Think carefully about your teacher's views. Your answer to this question should include if your teacher wants you to focus on specific information for a few main topics, if he wants you to know only some detail about many different ideas, or if he will be looking for some combination of these two. Your response should also include if your teacher is looking for you to memorize information, or if he would prefer for you to take what you have learned and apply it to a new and different context.

_____
_____
_____
_____
_____
_____
_____
_____

4. What information will be provided to you on the test?

Depending on the subject, your teacher may give you certain information on the test so that you do not have to memorize it. This usually includes mathematic or scientific formulas and equations. It may also include dates and names of places, or whatever else your teacher thinks is relevant but unnecessary for you to commit to memory. The fact that your teacher gives you this information means that he is planning to ask questions closely related to these topics.

_____
_____
_____
_____
_____
_____
_____

❖ **What to Review**

You now have on paper all the pieces of information you were able to gather about your exam. In this section we will put these pieces together to complete the puzzle.

Your answer to question #1 is the source from which you should spend the majority of your time studying. The source your teacher uses most to relay information to you is usually the same one he will turn to when it is time for him to make the test. If this source is something you have already outlined, such as your textbook readings, then you need not look much at it again. You can rely on your outline because it is essentially the source, just with all of the unnecessary information cut out of it. If you feel that your outline may be lacking in some regards or that the points on your outline have connecting information between them that you are failing to understand, you can always return to the source. At some point during your test preparation, it is a good idea to quickly skim the original source to ensure there is nothing you are missing. For question #1, make sure to consider your textbook, lecture notes, recent assignments and projects, handouts, and supplementary readings.

The purpose of question #2 is to acquaint yourself with the content and style of questions your teacher likes to use. The sources you identify in this response contain excellent practice questions for the test. Make sure you review old assignments and are able to answer questions from these sources. There are many different ways to ask a question. The specific ways your teacher has chosen to do so in past assignments gives you clues as to how the questions on your test will be formatted. If your teacher, for instance, tends to give you short answer questions for homework assignments, you can be pretty certain they are going to be popping up on the test. If you have access to previous versions of this test, make sure to look carefully at these as they are the best practice questions of all! You may be able to use your network and borrow old tests from previous students of the course.

Question #3 encourages you to define the scope of knowledge for which you are responsible. This heavily depends on your teacher. Some teachers just want to ask a few general questions that you can answer in essays, while others like to give multiple choice tests asking for detailed and specific information. Your answers to questions #1 and #2 give you insight into what texts you should study in addition to your notes and outlines. Your response to question #3, while no more than an estimate, may help you to decide the extent to which you should study the details of a specific topic.

Question #4 will not always be applicable. However, when it is, your response will be helpful in focusing you on the proper information. Any time your teacher announces that he will be giving you specific information on the test, make sure that you know how to use any related information so that you will be able to work with and explain the given facts. Additionally, your answer to question #4 will confirm the items that you need not memorize. If you know that a complex or obscure piece of information, such as a very long physics equation, will not be given on the test, you may want to ask your teacher if you need to memorize it. Sometimes, teachers bring up such items to help you conceptualize or understand other more important information and do not expect you to be able to recall the item on your own.

When you use these guiding questions, you will have a good idea of what your test will be like long before you lay eyes on it. With this knowledge, you can comfortably and adequately prepare for the upcoming test.

❖ **Where and with Whom**

Before we move on to all of the excitement in **How**, we need to take a moment to discuss the *who* and the *where* of studying. Students often like to make study groups or to study at a friend's house. Sometimes, students even like to have a sleepover study party. Students also have their choice of study locations: in a classroom at school, at the library, at home, at a café, or on the bus. With all these options available, you want to be sure to choose the ones that will best position you for success.

As far as study groups go, it is generally best to avoid them. Some consider the idea of a study group to be almost an oxymoron in and of itself (think *jumbo shrimp*)! Studying is for the individual, just as your test will be. Studying, therefore, is usually best carried out by an individual rather than a group. It is hard to bring the exciting topics and gossip to a halt and to return to focused studying when you are surrounded by a group of friends who would rather chat. No one can do the learning for you.

What a study group does provide you with is a group of students who may be able to answer any questions you have. Likewise, it provides you with a group of students whom you can teach. Teaching information to others will help you to understand the information better yourself. However, unless you have particular questions to ask other students or a specific desire for a student audience, a study group is not going to be very helpful. Furthermore, there are more reliable sources you can use to clarify any problems you have; remember to check your textbook, teacher, supplementary reading, notes, and handouts. Also, while teaching is an excellent way to familiarize yourself with a topic, it is generally best to do that one-on-one or in sessions that are solely meant for you to teach the other person. What's more, it is really only a good idea for you to teach test material once you have entirely completed all of your studying.

The one time when it would be most fit for a student to participate in a study group would be if he were entirely lost on his own and had many questions he needed to ask others shortly before the test. Then it would be beneficial for him to attend a study group of serious students who would be able to answer his questions. Other students, especially the more serious ones, are wary of being dragged down when they have a lot of their own studying to do. If you end up needing the help of others, you want the other students in the group to feel good about taking their time to help you. Make sure to offer your knowledge, notes, supplementary readings, outlines, and anything else that may be of service to others in the group. Most importantly, prepare for the group study session ahead of time so that you come prepared with specific questions and can be efficient with both your time and theirs.

It is important to study in an atmosphere that will allow you to concentrate on your work. Set yourself up for success by avoiding potential distractions. As we have already seen, working with a group of other students in a study group puts you in position to be taken off track. Likewise, studying near a television that is on or a computer with an instant messaging program running will interfere with your studies; have sufficient respect for yourself to avoid such distractions. Study where you know you will have peace and quiet so that you can think on your own about the material. The best and most well-equipped place for this is your study spot. If you have time to study while you are still at school, look for a vacant classroom or a secluded section in your school's library. If you are forced to study in a noisy and crowded study hall, try to score a seat away from everyone else, maybe even choose one facing a wall. It may not seem like the coolest place to sit, but as far as your success is concerned, it will definitely be the coolest seat in the house.

Maintain your smart attitude and positive confidence. What matters most to you is succeeding in school and achieving your goal. When it comes down to studying, follow your intuition. Make the choices that will help you to stay focused and achieve success. Limit your distractions and do what you can to learn from and teach yourself.

❖ How

This is the party section! Okay, well maybe it isn't exactly a party, but creating an effective study guide and using these memorization and test preparation techniques 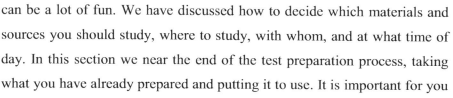 can be a lot of fun. We have discussed how to decide which materials and sources you should study, where to study, with whom, and at what time of day. In this section we near the end of the test preparation process, taking what you have already prepared and putting it to use. It is important for you to stay on the schedule you made for yourself in the **When** section so that you do not get off track. Here we will discuss the many fun techniques you can use to make understanding and memorizing the test material easier and more enjoyable for yourself.

Your attitude is invaluable when it comes to achieving success, and this is especially true when studying and preparing for a test. You need to have the positive attitude that you will succeed. Believing and having total conviction in the fact that you *will* be able to complete all of the studying and memorization that you need to makes a big difference in your studying. Do not get discouraged or think negative thoughts. Focus only on positives: you *can* figure out the answer; you *will* understand that difficult concept. Your mind will more easily accept and try to understand information if it knows that it is capable of doing so.

As you progress in your studies, confidently complete each item that is part of your study plan. Once you have finished studying an item, such as your notes on a particular topic, you should not need to go over that item again. Add to your outline any information of which you do not yet have a firm grasp; we will soon discuss this further. A day or two before the test, you may choose to review some sources in full, such as reading all of your notes and not only the highlighted areas, so as to refresh any smaller points for yourself.

Before you begin studying, you may find it beneficial to spend a little time meditating. Sit in a comfortable position, and close your eyes. Relax, and don't think about anything except for the fact that you are going to spend the next several hours studying for your test. Envision how easily you will absorb, understand, and memorize the information. Be positive about spending time studying. Think of some of the topics you are interested in and are glad you have learned. Also, take this time to recognize that studying is an excellent and important use of your time, and connect it to the fact that this is what will get you that top grade on your upcoming test and ultimately lead you to your goal. Imagine how good you will feel taking the test and knowing all of the answers because you studied so well and with confidence, and picture your teacher handing you back your test with an excellent mark.

Starting off your study session with a few minutes of relaxation and confidence-boosting self-talk has been shown to result in a more pleasant and productive study period.

While preparing for your test, be sure to review any graded assignments you have relating to the test material, including past homework problems, quizzes, projects, and other assignments. These can serve as great guides to point your study sessions in the right direction. Look at any items you got wrong or found confusing. You may notice a common theme running between the content of your incorrect answers. Write down those topics you identify for further review. Also make a note on your outline of any repeated careless errors, such as if you kept forgetting to change the units on a problem before applying a specific equation. This way, during the test, you can make a point to avoid those careless errors you made in the past.

o **Creating a Study Guide**

Your classroom notes and reading outlines are extremely valuable to your studying. Your outline initially contained any important information from your reading assignments. In class, you had the option of adding important notes directly to your outline as well. The final step to transform your outline into a comprehensive study guide is to add certain highlighted sections of information from your daily note review sessions.

You will do this shortly before your exam, usually at least three days ahead of time. That should get you close enough to the exam date so that you will have all or almost all of the necessary information highlighted in your notes. It will also give you a few days to get good use out of your new study guide.

Don't worry; you will by no means be adding *all* of your highlighted notes. By this point, you will have checked off the majority of the highlights on your notes, handouts, and other materials. The remaining highlighted information is what you will add to your outline. Choose the information you add carefully. Even if the information is highlighted, if you feel that you do not need to study it further, leave it out.

You can add this new information to your outline under the proper Roman numeral headings if there is room. I usually find that there is not enough space on the front and instead add the information to the blank backside of the outline pages. By adding the information to the back of your pages, you will have plenty of room to organize the additional information under proper headings. Just as you numerically ordered your outline, you can similarly organize the new information under clearly demarcated headings. As you add the information, keep your writing compact. Write your notes here as you do in class, making use of shorthand and cutting out unnecessary words.

This modified outline will serve as your complete study guide for the test. It is great to make the study guide just before the weekend so that you have a couple of days to get full use out of your study guide. Also, while preparing for your test and reviewing the sources brought up by the four questions, you may very well want to add other information to your study guide. If, for example, while preparing for your history exam you spot an important date that you have had trouble remembering and that is not already on your outline, go ahead and add it. When you study your souped-up outline, you will be learning the information *you* need to know for the test.

Read over your outline and study material frequently. If you have several outlines you made for multiple reading assignments related to a test, clip the outlines together. When you add new information, try to group it with the outline that is most similar content-wise.

Your study guide will be easy to carry around with you and will not take an inordinate amount of time to review. It is to your benefit to study it frequently. I recommend you photocopy your study guide so that you can transport it without worrying about losing or damaging your only copy. When it comes to the point that you know certain information on your study guide well, check those items off so that you do not waste your time restudying information you already know.

   o **Over Twenty Techniques for Comprehension and Retention**

Now we arrive at the nitty-gritty of the study process: mentally organizing and memorizing the test material. Included in this section are over twenty techniques and some clever variations that will enable you to memorize the required material and to enjoy doing it. Once you understand the material, the following three simple steps are necessary in order to employ a memorization technique.

Steps to Employing a Study Technique

1. Select the technique you like best for the specific information.
2. Apply the technique to the information. Take the time to correctly format and mentally connect the two. Be sure the connection is well ingrained in your mind before you move on.
3. As you continue in your studies, periodically recall the memorized information to make sure you still remember it and to further embed it in your mind. For example, practice recalling information before you go to sleep at night, on the bus, during a television commercial, in the lunchroom, or in study hall. This is the best way to ensure that you will be able to recall the necessary knowledge when you need to. There is a big difference between being able to identify information and actually being able to think of it on your own.

Studying for most tests requires you to commit information to memory. Thanks to your daily review sessions, outlines, and persistent hard work, you have a thorough understanding of the material you need to memorize. The only question now is how you will be able to get the information down well enough to be able to recall it during your test.

It all begins with choosing an appropriate study technique. As promised, the following pages are filled with unique and effective memorization methods to propel you towards success on your test. This is clearly quite a large selection of study methods. You don't need to use all of them or to memorize them. Choose those that you like best and that work well with the specific content you need to know for a certain test. Keep this book handy whenever you study so that you will be able to quickly look for and select a good memorization method no matter what the topic at hand. As you read through this list now, put an asterisk next to those methods you like best. This way it will be easier for you to identify your favorites when you come back to this list in the future.

Top Comprehension and Retention Techniques

• **Examples:** Just as it is often easier to understand a concept with an example, it is often easier to remember something with an example. This is especially true for science courses. For instance, as you will learn in chemistry, when liquid droplets evaporate from a surface, the surface cools. This is because energy is being transferred from the surface to the droplets, heating them so that they evaporate. Instead of memorizing these facts, simply connect them to an example. Your body sweats in order to cool itself; as you may have noticed, when droplets of sweat evaporate from your skin, your body releases heat. It is much easier to "memorize" an example you understand well than an esoteric set of facts. Make sure to ask your teacher for an example whenever you need one.

• **Acronyms:** An acronym is a word or word-like group of letters formed from the first letter of several words. Acronyms are very useful and are popular among students of all ages. Common examples of acronyms include the words *laser* and *scuba*, standing for *light amplification by the stimulated emission of radiation* and *self-contained underwater breathing apparatus*, respectively, as well as the word *NATO*, standing for *North Atlantic Treaty Organization*. Acronyms do not even have to spell out words. They can simply be a set of letters, such as is the case with the *NCAA*, or *National Collegiate Athletic Association*, and the *WNBA*, or *Women's National Basketball Association*. You can apply acronyms to various types of information that you may have to memorize. They are especially of use when you need to remember the order of a process or event. A good example of using an acronym is for the process of cell division, known as mitosis. Mitosis occurs with the following phases in sequential order: prophase, metaphase, anaphase, and telophase. To remember this, I simply remember the acronym *PMAT*. Another common example is the acronym for the colors of the rainbow, *ROY G. BIV*, which, in order from the top of the arch to the bottom, stands for *red, orange, yellow, green, blue,* and *indigo violet*.

- **Sentences:** Similar to acronyms, sentences can be used to help you memorize sequential information. Instead of using the first letter of each word to make a word, though, you will make a sentence. Sentences are especially useful when the letters you have to use do not form a good acronym, although they do add the burden of requiring you to memorize an entire sentence instead of a simple word. A common example of this method is *My Dear Aunt Sally*, which stands for the mathematical order of operations in which one must *multiply* and *divide* before *adding* and *subtracting*.

- **Alphabetizing:** Often, a series of information can be advantageously arranged in alphabetical order, either in the forward or reverse direction. This is best shown with an example. Say you will be expected to know the size differences between various wavelengths of light, including that *infrared waves* are shorter than *microwaves*, which are shorter than *radio waves*. You already know that *I* comes before *M*, which comes before *R*, so you can simply remember that that the wavelengths increase in length in this same order. Then, when you get to the test, you will be able to arrange the sizes of the wavelengths in their correct order. I find this technique to be quite useful and adaptable to many different subject areas.

- **Relations:** Sometimes, we have our own unique connecting factors that we can put to use for our studies. When I was in third grade, I had to memorize the capitals of all fifty states. As soon as I learned that Frankfort is the capital of Kentucky, I thought of KFC (the restaurant chain named *Kentucky Fried Chicken*—watch those acronyms!). When you study, relations such as these may pop out at you even if they don't work for other people. You are a unique person with your own rich life experiences. Take advantage of them whenever you can, including when you are studying. If while working, an idea suddenly pops out at you—*hey, this reminds me of…*—use that (odd) little connection to help you remember the new information.

- **Size:** Size is often an aspect in terms of facts you have to memorize for class. At times, you may be able to connect the physical sizes of the words themselves with the items they describe. For example, the *endoplasmic reticulum* is a large organelle found in the cell. You can remember this because its name is also pretty large. Another large organelle, but somewhat smaller than the endoplasmic reticulum, is the *Golgi apparatus*. It has a long name, but still a shorter name than the endoplasmic reticulum. *Lysosomes* are smaller than either of these other organelles, and likewise there are fewer letters in the word *lysosomes*. This technique can be used in many situations, including those cases in which you will need to label a diagram. By looking at a depiction of a cell, for instance, you will be able to tell which item is the endoplasmic reticulum simply by its large size.

- **Pictures:** As you know, *a picture says a thousand words*. For the sake of your studying, this can come in use. Instead of separately studying and memorizing each individual detail of a concept, you can remember a picture that allows you to see the information clearly. Say you need to memorize what surface tension is and the surface tension characteristics of water. Surface tension is a measure of how difficult

  it is to stretch or break the surface of a liquid; water has a relatively high surface tension. To remember this, you can picture the photograph shown to the right, in which a water strider is able to walk across a pond thanks to the surface  tension of water. Recalling this image will enable you to apply and understand the concept of surface tension.

- **Path:** The path technique involves matching a series of facts with a familiar routine. This technique is most useful for memorizing concepts that have multiple ordered steps. For instance, a science class may require you to know the scientific method in the following order: problem, hypothesis, experiment, analysis, and conclusion. To apply the path technique, select a location and routine you know well, such as your walk to gym class at school or going from your bedroom to the mailbox at home. Following through with the gym class example, say on your way to gym you go through the school lobby, then pass the cafeteria, the main office, and the locker room, in that order, and then finally you arrive at the gymnasium. Connect the places involved in this routine to the components of the scientific method in their respective order. Engage your different senses to make your path a realistic experience. When you walk into the school lobby, imagine a big bright red banister that says *PROBLEM*. As you go by the cafeteria, smell what's cooking for lunch. When you can't quite place the aroma, glance at today's lunch menu, which says at the top *HYPOTHESIS Hamburgers*. They always serve such weird things in school cafeterias. Next, go by the school's main office. Maybe you are surprised to see the door shut and lights off. There is a sign on the door that says in bold black letters: Closed for *EXPERIMENT*. You're not really sure what that's all about, but you don't want to be late for gym so you keep going. When you get to the locker room your gym teacher informs you that today the Physical Education department is conducting its yearly fitness *ANALYSIS*. That's going to be a tough workout, so you go to your locker and get out your gym clothes. After you are done changing you go into the gym to do your workout. You are looking forward to its *CONCLUSION*. This is a clever method of memorization and it can be fun to form a path for the information. Make sure to be creative and add enough detail so that recalling the information will be as easy as a walk in the park (or at least as a walk to gym class).

- **Self-quiz:** The self-quiz is an excellent way for you to review the test material. Once you have studied a topic, make a quiz for yourself. To do this, you can look at old assignments or textbook problems related to the topic and write down a few questions to then answer. Another method is to take a blank piece of paper and write down a few key words and ideas related to the topic; then, spend time recalling and writing down all of the information that these key words bring to mind. If you expect your test to contain mostly essay questions, as is common in the humanities, think about and identify the main ideas your teacher has been trying to get across. With these in mind, write down relevant essay questions that you would ask if you were the teacher, and make sure you can come up with a good answer for each question. Try to write everything you know and can remember for each item, whether it be in response to a question or a key word from the list of ideas you created. If a friend or family member is around, you can give him or her your list of questions and key words and have that individual quiz you on the information.

Having someone else quiz you works particularly well for questions that call for short and specific answers, such as vocabulary translations between two languages. You may do really well on the self-quiz, or you may not. If you don't, take note of your problem areas. These are clearly items that you will need to study further. If you get every question right on your self-quiz, then that shows you have a good understanding of the topic. Either way, do not become stressed. The self-quiz is not meant to be a prediction of how well you will do on your actual test but rather is a study aid meant to enhance your familiarity with the test material.

- **Repetition:** Many people find that various forms of repetition help them to remember information. You should choose those methods which work best for you. Some students like to write the information over and over. When it comes time for the test, they remember writing down the information about which the test questions are asking. Others like to read the information aloud over and over again. During the test, they can remember speaking out the words. Oral repetition is especially helpful for subjects that deal with large or unusual words; you will better remember these words and their meanings if you say them aloud. The most common way people memorize information is by looking at and reading it over silently many times. This particularly comes in use when memorizing exact definitions and straight forward facts. Focus on each piece of information and let it become ingrained in your mind. Recite the information silently in your head in a calm and relaxed voice. Your mind is much more absorbent when you treat it kindly and talk to it in a gentle voice than when you become frustrated and try bluntly forcing information on it.

- **Recording:** It can be helpful to make a simple tape, CD, or MP3 recording of yourself saying aloud the information you want to memorize. Since this method often requires a good deal of preparation time, it is most appropriate to use for long-term studying. You can then listen to the information whenever you want, such as while exercising, walking, or travelling in the car. Hearing yourself speak the information over and over again reinforces the information in your mind. Some people even believe that it is beneficial to listen to recordings while sleeping. To make the recording, all you need is an inexpensive microphone you can hook up to your computer. You can then record yourself and transfer the soundtrack to a CD or MP3

> *A sleep learning study conducted at Duke University divided forty students into two groups. As a baseline, both groups were tested for their ability to remember words under normal circumstances. The following day, they were to be tested on a second set of words. The second list of words was played to one group while sleeping. The next day, both groups were taught the new words. The sleep-trained group had a significantly higher retention rate, leading the study to conclude that there is "retention of auditory material presented during sleep."*

player. Or, you can directly record yourself onto a tape using a tape recorder. A recording can be of excellent use in memorizing a long list of vocabulary words, such as you may need to do for the SAT or for an English final exam. In such cases, I would recommend you make a recording of yourself saying each word and then defining it. After saying each vocabulary word, pause for a moment. When listening to the tape later, this will give you a chance to think of the definition on your own before hearing it. If a recording will take you a particularly long time to make, you may want to break it up over time. For instance, in the case of recording vocabulary words and definitions for an English final exam, it would be a good idea to record the words throughout the semester as you learn them rather than waiting until closer to the final. Before you make a recording, consider if you will have enough time to use it later so that you are sure it will be of benefit to you.

- **Review Sheet:** Using a review sheet to study from is one of the best and most useful ways to study, and it is my personal favorite. Most often, you will be studying from your outline or prepared study guide. A day or two before the test, if you find your study guide is cluttered with information that you already know well, take a sheet of paper out and add only those items you still need to review. Then you can look at each piece of information on its own and memorize it until you have completed the entire sheet. This is a very useful method, especially because of how quick it is to make and how easily portable it is. As usual, if you plan to carry it around with you, I recommend that you photocopy the original. When studying from a review sheet, it is often helpful to cover information and then to try and recall it on your own. While studying for Spanish class, for instance, you can write the Spanish vocabulary on the left side of the page and the English translations on the right. Then, cover either one and figure out the translation of the word left uncovered.

- **Flashcards:** Flashcards are similar to using a review sheet but take more time and effort on your part. I have heard students say on countless occasions, *I made flashcards, but I didn't have a chance to study them!* This is all too true. In many instances, flashcards require more preparation time than they are worth. A piece of paper on which you can momentarily cover and then uncover information with your hand can usually work as well as flipping a flashcard, but it does not require the large amount of preparatory time. Furthermore, flashcards are easily lost, and a couple missing flashcards could result in missing points on a test. If you find that flashcards would really be beneficial in a specific instance, make sure you really have the time to make them *and* to study them. Number the flashcards in the upper right hand corner so that you can easily check to see if any are missing. Also, write the number of the last flashcard somewhere on the bottom of the first flashcard so that you will be able to tell if you lose the last flashcard in the set. It is best to use smaller cards that will be easier to transport, such as the 3" x 5" size rather than the 4" x 6" dimensions, and to write with a pen that does not go through the paper since you will want to write on both sides of the note card. Many note cards are lined on one side and blank on the other. On the blank side, write the key word, idea, or image you need to know about and identify. On the lined side write the relevant details. To use the cards, look at the key word and try to recall all the information you can about it. Afterwards, check the other side of the card to see if you have all of your facts right. Later on, you can try reading all the facts on one side and guessing the key word they describe. Depending on the nature of the information, you may choose to do those two steps in the reverse order. Flashcards are especially useful for memorizing vocabulary words and their definitions, dates in history and their significance, and pictures of artwork or other items that you will be responsible for identifying. In the last situation, you can use the blank sides of the card to draw the pictures, such as the different phases a cell goes through during mitosis (cell division), and then write the name of the phase and its characteristics on the lined side. One great thing about flashcards is that they make it easy for someone else to test you or for you to test yourself. Again, please allow me to stress that you should only put in the effort to make flashcards if you will have the time to use them. Otherwise, put the information on a review sheet and save yourself unnecessary time and trouble.

- **Implications:** Often, you can deduce what you need to know from information that you already know or that your teacher gives you on the test. This is often true with mathematical type expressions, such as physics equations. For instance, in physics, the equation to find the final velocity (v_f) of an object at constant acceleration (a) is equal to the initial velocity (v_i) plus the product of its acceleration and the total time elapsed (t). In short, the equation is $v_f = v_i + at$. Besides memorizing the equation and knowing where to plug in the numbers you are given on the test, you want to understand this equation on a fundamental level. Students often forget that such equations are not simply magical formulas that spit out the correct answer, but rather they are grounded in concepts that are logical and apparent in the surrounding world. This means that there is information that you can deduce from this equation. Therefore, you do not need to memorize anything further than that small equation, $v_f = v_i + at$, to make some of the following observations. For one, the equation tells us that the final velocity of an object that is positively accelerating will be greater than the initial velocity, with the magnitude of that difference being dependant on the total time of acceleration. Furthermore, you can derive the units of acceleration from this expression because *at* must have the same units of velocity, and therefore the units of acceleration are simply those of velocity divided by time. Take a moment to see how these deductions can be made. When you learn a new equation, always take the time to think about its implications. Many test questions that seem complicated are basically asking for something you can derive from an equation or idea that you already know. These questions often ask about certain fundamental ideas that in fact can be directly derived from a given concept.

- **Equations:** Equations can be used in many creative ways to help you memorize information. You can format your equation to fit whatever it is you need to memorize. Equations are great for defining concrete facts, such as the fact that King Henry VIII had six wives, or simply *H8=6*. Condensing the information in this way will cut down on the words you need to memorize and keep things short and sweet. Choose the variables and symbols that are easiest for you to remember.

- **Song:** Most people really love to sing, especially when no one else is around. This is great for your studies because songs have an odd way of sticking with us, getting stuck in our heads even when we don't want them around! You can use this to your advantage. Condense the information you need to memorize into as few words as reasonably possible, leaving out any little extras that don't matter, and then throw in some of your own original ideas and lyrics to make the song work. Match your lyrics to a tune you like. The words don't need to rhyme, just use a memorable beat. It can be a kids' song, such as *Row, Row, Row Your Boat*, or your favorite song off the radio. Sing your new song over and over. You may even want to make a recording of it and listen to it when you are commuting or doing housework. Also, check out YouTube for songs other students have made to help themselves study. They may give you ideas for your song or you may choose to use one of theirs. In the YouTube search box, type the specific topic of interest followed by the word *song*. For instance, to find a song about mitosis (cell division), I would type *mitosis song* into the search box. It will be fun to create and learn your new song, and it will enable easier recall of the information during your test. Who knows, you may do so well with this method that your classmates will be asking you for a copy of your album... and your autograph!

- **Poetry:** Making information into rhyming verses can be just as helpful to the memory as singing it. The rhyme of the verses will wake up your mind to the information just as the beat of the music does. Rhymes are sometimes harder to make, but many students have a good time writing short poems. It is easier to remember a rhyme than a bland piece of information. When you spice up your studying with rhyming verses, you will be able to recall information with more ease, and it will make study time a breeze!

- **Visualization:** The use of visualizing information is different than the picture method we discussed earlier. With the picture method, you were to make a picture in your mind of an example of a certain idea or principle at work. Visualization is different in that it involves you picturing the information itself rather than an example of it. Because of this, visualization is best applied to information that has a picture to offer, such as a historical event or a description of a character in an English class novel. If you are going to be tested on the literary work you read for English class, for instance, sit down and visualize the main characters. If one of the boys in the story was mean, give him a menacing face. Lazy? Picture him with droopy eyelids. Visualize each character in detail in your mind: pretty, ugly, fat, skinny, rich, poor, tall, short, etc. When you come to a test question on the description of a character, you will be able to answer it by visualizing the character in your mind. Make the details clear in your vision. You may actually prefer to draw a picture of the character in order to ensure that you have a clear view of him or her in your mind. History can be studied in the same way. If in class you learn about a specific war that took place, picture the fighting factions in their proper uniforms. Were there any key figures your teacher stressed in class? If so, then make sure to include them and how they died, or didn't die, or whatever was unique about them, in the still or moving picture you create in your mind.

- **Color:** Research has shown that colors can help us to remember information. Try using color on your study sheet, flashcards, or outline. Use a specific color for a specific topic of information; when you get to the next topic, change colors. This will help your mind to group related information together. Later on, while doing further studying and even while taking your test, if you stop and focus on the applicable color, you may better be able to recall the information for that specific topic. I often will make my study sheet using fine point markers or colored pens or pencils in an assortment of colors. This makes creating the study sheet more interesting and makes the sheet itself look more attractive. Furthermore, I have actually found that while taking my test I am able at times to see in my mind something I wrote on my study sheet in its color form.

- **Teaching:** It is often said that we learn best by teaching. When you teach something, you are forced to present the material in a way that is both clear and logical. In your presentation, you will be filling in gaps of information for yourself that you may have not even considered before. Furthermore, others may ask you questions that will require you to think about the concept from new angles. If you are working on memorizing and further understanding a new concept or idea, teach the information to someone else, be it your friend, parent, or sibling. This is a great tool for helping you in your studies and for allowing someone else to learn something new.

These are all tried and true techniques that make studying and memorizing information fun and interesting. Remember to put the method you select to work for you. You may want to throw in extra details to the path story you are creating, including all the senses you can, or to mold the lyrics of your self-composed song to a popular beat on the radio. Creatively match these methods to your personal tastes in order to make them work their best for you.

At this point in the process, you will have learned, understood, studied, memorized, and tested yourself on all the information you need to know for your exam. These steps are to be carried out on the days leading up to your test. The day before the test itself, as you may recall, will be left free so that you will have time to review your outlines and to clear up and further study any remaining points of confusion. This last day is also a good time for you to narrow down your study guide to the particular information on which you still need to focus for the exam.

Make sure to put your study guide and any review sheets you made to use. Keep them close at hand and study them whenever you get the chance. If there is a specific piece of information that you are having trouble remembering, you can bring your review sheet with you to the test and look at it right before the exam begins. Then, as soon as the test begins, you can quickly jot down the information on your test or scrap paper. It is best to write the information in pencil or erasable pen so that you can erase it before you hand your test in; or you can write it in a discreet area, such as on the back of one of the test pages, to keep your test from looking messy. This will allow you to take the rest of the test not having to worry about recalling the information with which you were having trouble.

❖ **Your Final Hours**

The evening before your test, before getting ready for bed, prepare everything that you will need physically with you during the exam. You may need a calculator, equation sheet, water bottle, tissue pack, pen, pencil, eraser, or other items. Go ahead and put these in your book bag so that you will not forget to bring them in the morning. It is a good idea to wear your digital watch on test day so that you can keep track of how much time you have during the exam. Also, go ahead and pick out what you are going to wear. You want to have on something that you are confident and comfortable in, so you can move freely and concentrate entirely on your test.

It is important that you get enough sleep the night before the test. Your sleep impacts your test score. When your mind is more rested it is more alert, better at spotting trick questions, and more efficient at thinking of the correct answer. After you are totally ready for and in bed, try looking over your review sheet (page 120) or study guide one last time for the day. While you are asleep, your mind processes and memorizes the information it has received throughout the day. Give your mind this one last boost of the information you want it to go over.

Once you shut off the lights, let your mind go blank and relax. You can also meditate on the idea of having a good night's rest and on your subconscious brain processing all of the important information you studied during the day. The quality of your sleep is very important. Tell your mind and body that you want to feel well-rested and alert when you wake up in the morning. If you concentrate on this before trying to fall asleep, your body will most likely comply. It helps you to do better on your test when you wake up feeling strong and refreshed.

When you get up in the morning, start with a positive attitude. Be excited for the test you are going to take. This is the culmination of all of your hard work. This is your chance to prove yourself and to show what a successful student you really are. As far as your morning routine goes, do not break habit. Eat a nutritious, low sugar, high protein breakfast. If you never eat breakfast, don't make test day into an experiment, but do at some point make breakfast part of your routine; it is good for you in so many ways. Your diet has an effect on your brain and overall well-being.

If necessary, you can use your trip to school and any other spare time on test day to do some last-minute studying. Arrive to class early, and, if possible, choose a seat positioned where you are comfortable working. It may be near the heater, away from the fan, far from a cheater, or in the front of the room where nothing will be in front of you to distract you. After making your choice, sit down and prepare your area for the test. Get out whatever materials you will need to have during the exam and put everything else away except for your review sheet. Go over your review sheet for the rest of the remaining time. If you have any questions on the material you are studying, this is your last chance to ask your teacher. At this point, do not make the mistake of thinking any question is too small, stupid, or irrelevant. You have been studying hard and still have these questions to ask. Clearly, they do not have obvious answers. For some unfortunate reason, it always seems as if those questions I wanted to ask but didn't always end up on the test. Please, learn from my mistakes and take advantage of your last opportunity to ask your teacher about any problems you have! If you are comfortable with what you know and do not need to talk to your teacher, then you can keep reading over your review sheet if you want. If you have more information to study, don't stop for any distractions, even when other students start filling up the room, making noise, and studying aloud for the test. Keep going over the information you need to know until your teacher insists everyone puts away study material so that the exam may begin.

Finally, when you get that test, start it with confidence, with a sense of accomplishment, and with pride. You know the material for that test inside out. Because you answered the four predicting questions, you have a good idea about what the test will be like. You studied all the necessary information and memorized what you needed to. You practiced recalling the information and tested yourself on the material. You are golden and good to go. Think positive thoughts; take a good solid deep inhalation and then exhale and relax before you even look down at the paper. You know you can do well, and it is time to show it. *You may begin!*

Taking the Test

You have come down to the final test. All the time you spent reading, taking notes, reviewing, studying, and memorizing has been directed toward preparing yourself for this exam. You know all the information. Now, it is only a matter of using it to answer each question correctly. For some students, this is the hardest part of all. Nobody likes to get a test back and see missed points as a result of incorrectly answering questions to which he or she really did know the answer. This section is focused on ensuring that such a scenario never happens to you in the future. The ideas we will go into are practical, easy to understand, and, most importantly, will have a notable impact on your test score. Make sure you understand the main points of each section. Also, this would be a good time to review all of the chapter summaries up to this point. Doing so will help keep things fresh in your mind and in the proper perspective.

❖ **Testing Techniques**

Tests really test you on much more than the information your teacher wants you to know. They test you on your capability to understand what the question is asking, to apply what you know to figure out the answer, and to give the correct answer in the appropriate format. Most teachers only allow you a certain amount of time in which you can work on your test, and therefore your test is also testing your ability to do all of the above in a time efficient manner. Here, we will discuss the best general techniques so that you can meet and surpass these demands.

I recommend that you use an erasable pen or pencil for your test. Pencil with #2 lead is preferable unless you are required to use pen. With a pencil, you will be prepared to fill out any sheets that may require pencil, and you will also be able to cleanly erase any mistakes. Be careful to write darkly enough with the pencil that your teacher will not have trouble seeing it. If you must use pen, use an erasable pen for the same reasons a pencil is preferable. Make sure to pack these items the night before the test. It is a good idea to always keep an extra set of these writing utensils in your locker as well. It is also helpful to have an extra eraser that works well, just in case you need it.

As we have discussed before, it is important that you are calm while taking your test. Keep your mind relaxed and clear and ready to give you the answers you need. Before you even look at your test, take a moment to calm yourself. Take a deep breath, clear your mind of irrelevant thoughts, and relieve yourself of any tension by lowering your shoulders and relaxing your jaw and forehead. Sit up straight with both your feet solidly planted on the floor. With this calm and relaxed position, your mind will be able to think more clearly during your test. You will be physically alert and mentally at your best.

The first thing you should do when you look at your test is to briefly skim the entire exam. You need to know what lies ahead so that you can be prepared and budget your time accordingly. If your test is only one page, make sure to check the back of it. I have seen students totally neglect the back side of their test, and others who realized there was a backside with only minutes left in the testing period. Take note of the question types and demands. Usually, you will want to do your test in the order it was written. When applicable, I sometimes prefer to get the easier portions of the test over with first, such as doing the multiple choice section before the essay questions, as doing so may provide some clues for the harder sections and will help put me in the proper frame of mind. This is really up to you because only you know what you feel more comfortable doing first. Your strategy for the test should revolve around getting the most points possible. Avoid skipping around looking to do the easiest questions first; wasting a lot of your precious time triaging the test questions will not help your grade.

One of the most obvious things students tend to overlook is the directions. Always read through the directions before you start to work on a particular section. Usually directions will say what you expect them to, but sometimes they can surprise you. They may tell you to answer only four of the six questions or that some multiple choice questions have more than one answer. Skipping over the directions could cause you to do an entire section incorrectly or to miss out on easy points.

As far as speed goes, you need to be quick but accurate. Keep in mind that you are under time pressure. If there is a specific question that you cannot think of the answer to, give it your best guess, put a little question mark (?) in the margin so you know to come back to it, and keep going. You don't want one question to take up time you could use to answer several questions. What's more, as you continue working, you may be reminded of the answer that you need for the skipped problem. In **When You Don't Know**, we will discuss what to do when you cannot think of the answer to a problem.

As the test progresses, some of the other students may become restless. They may tap their pencils, go back and forth to the teacher's desk for help, make frequent trips to the restroom, or do something else distracting. Don't let these disturbances get to you. Focus only on yourself and your test. If someone else finishes the test early, or even if many others finish early, don't let it distract you or make you nervous. Keep working at a good pace with a positive attitude, answering each question carefully and with thought.

If something is unclear to you in the directions or in a specific question, it is important to ask the teacher. You do not want to get points off for a misunderstanding. After deciding to go to your teacher for help, make sure to get his or her attention quietly. Your teacher is more likely to help you if your doing so doesn't draw the attention of the entire class. Raise your hand to speak with your teacher, and speak softly. Make sure to ask something that will be easy and allowable for him or her to answer and at the same time that will be of use to you. One of the most helpful questions to ask a teacher during a test is if he or she could rephrase or reword the question for you. *Rephrase* is perfect

A Quiz on Following Directions

Directions: You have 5 minutes to complete this quiz. Carefully read all steps before doing anything.

1) Write today's full date on the top right hand corner of this page.
2) Beneath the date, write your full name.
3) Circle the word 'name' in the second sentence.
4) Add the numbers 928+87, and write the answer on the following line. _____
5) Write the name of the current president of the United States on the top left corner of this page.
6) Circle all of the vowels in the president's name.
7) Write "I am good at following directions" directly above the directions.
8) Mark your paper with a large 'A' for doing such a good job following directions. You deserve it.
9) Take your answer from line #4 and subtract 100. Write your new total directly beneath your old answer.
10) In the lower left hand corner, draw a picture of your favorite animal saying "This test is fun and easy."
11) Draw a smiley face above the animal's head. ☺
12) Write the names of your immediate family members on the bottom right corner of the page.
13) Think of an even number between 2 and 52. Double that number; add 28; subtract 9. Divide the result by two, and write your answer on the following line. _____
14) Now that you have carefully read all parts so far and not actually carried out any of the written work, skip the remaining part of the exam. Go back and complete only parts #7 and #8. Then, you are done.
15) Don't read the last line before reading the directions!

because your teacher will see that you need him to change the wording in the directions or in a question for your understanding, but that you are not trying to get the answer out of him. Meanwhile, wording the question this way does give your teacher the opportunity to give you a hint if he feels so inclined.

Finally, before handing in your test, make sure that you answered each question correctly. Providing you have time, always check over your test at least once before handing it in. If your test includes a Scantron sheet, then the first thing to check is that the answer choices on your test paper match the choices you entered on your Scantron sheet. Double-check that when you meant to fill in multiple choice letter *C* for problem #3, that you filled in choice *C* and not accidentally choice *D* in its place. Also check that you didn't mistakenly forget to fill in a blank after doing all the work to figure out an answer to a problem. Lastly, make sure that you properly lined up your answers on the Scantron with the proper question numbers. Often students become one question off and end up, for instance, placing #20's answer on #19, #21's on #20, and so on. After quickly checking that you filled in your answers the way you meant to, it is time to make sure that you came up with your answers correctly.

The best way to double-check your answers is to go through the whole test again, figuring out each answer without looking at your previous solution. Only do this once you have completed the entire test. If you have any problems labeled with question marks, attend to those before double-checking the rest of your exam. Starting at the beginning of the test, read each question and, without looking at your response, figure out what the answer should be. Then, check that your new answer matches your original response. You should always answer every question, even if it is only a guess. The only exception is in the case of an exam that penalizes guessing, such as the SAT. If additional points will be taken off for an incorrect answer as opposed to a blank answer, do not put down a guess unless you are able to narrow the answer choices down.

Once you have completed your double-checking, make sure to use the remaining time to ensure that you have answered each question correctly and to the best of your ability. Students often feel frustrated after spending a lot of time on their exam and just want to hand it in and leave.

> *"We don't get to the finish line and stop. That's when we give it even more than we started with."*
> -Jillian Michaels, fitness expert

Don't let this tempting downfall overtake you. Use your remaining test time productively to ensure your grade will be the best it can be. You want to answer every question you can correctly to maximize your score.

❖ **Understanding the Question**

To answer a question, you have to know what it is asking you. As is the nature of tests, occasionally some of the test questions will be difficult to understand. In this section, you will learn some pointers, definitions, and guidelines for how to handle such situations.

If you cannot figure out what a question is asking, skip the problem at first and put a question mark in the margin. As you continue working on the test, you will probably find other questions you may need to ask about. This way, instead of constantly getting up and down to bother your teacher for help, you can wait and ask several questions at once.

Our lovely language provides teachers with all sorts of words to use to test us on information. Sometimes, it can be a little confusing as to exactly what your teacher wants to know. Below are the meanings of the most common terms your teacher will use on a test. Read through them and make sure the definitions make sense to you. If any of the words are ambiguous, take a moment to review and familiarize yourself with the correct definitions. By no means do you have to memorize the exact definition of all of the words listed below; rather, you should have a general understanding of them in case they appear on a test.

Test Words to Know

➢ **Analyze** – break the topic up into its pieces and explain the pieces and their relevance to one another; you should also include how they fit together to make the whole

➢ **Compare** – examine and note the similarities and differences between two or more items

➢ **Contrast** – show the differences between two or more items

➢ **Critique** – analyze while providing specific criticism and evaluation of the pieces of the whole and the whole itself

> **Define** – give the definition or explain the meaning of a concept; these questions often want details and examples included in the response

> **Describe** – provide characteristics and features of an item

> **Discuss** – investigate by reasoning or argument; present in detail for examination or consideration

> **Evaluate** – determine the significance or condition of an item through careful study

> **Explain** – make the topic logically and plainly understandable

> **Justify** – prove or show an idea to be reasonable

> **State** – express the particulars of an item

> **Summarize** – give a condensed overview with the same general meaning

> **Trace** – follow in detail the path an object or idea went through over time in a step-by-step explanation

> _____

> _____

> _____

These tend to be the most common test words teachers use. If any others come to mind, you should look them up and add them to the list above. There are always those teachers who have their own unique and interesting vocabulary. If your teacher uses an unusual word once, he or she will likely use it again. Add the word to the list above so that you will be prepared the next time you encounter that expression.

❖ **Answering the Question**

You want to correctly answer each and every question you come across. Just like it can be tempting at times to hand in your test early and get it over with, it can also be tempting to not give your all for a response and to quickly continue on. Even if you become tired during the test, keep going. Each question counts. Try adopting the following attitude. Think of each question as a life and death situation. You are the doctor, and one small mistake will harm your patient. Put all your attention into coming up with the right answer. Your patient's well-being, or really your success, depends upon you getting this answer correct. There is no room for error or misunderstanding. Make sure you think of all the options available to you. You can't decide on one answer without considering other relevant options; then you may not be giving your patient the best antidote, or your teacher the best answer. A poor performance can hinder your success. Every question matters and requires your careful thought and attention.

Following in this line of thinking, you should have a reason that proves you are correct for each answer. Imagine that you got your test back and the teacher marked the problem you are working on as incorrect. Think how you would justify your answer to him or her. Know in your mind exactly what makes your answer correct and any other possibilities wrong.

Once you have answered a question, check to be sure you answered the *right* question. Often, teachers will ask you to solve for an item and then to adjust the answer somewhat. For example, you may have solved for how much *one* vanilla-frosted strawberry cupcake costs, while the question actually asked you to find how much *three* of these cupcakes cost. Always reread the question after you answer it to make sure you really did answer it correctly. If when you first read the question, even before you begin working on it, you notice a modifier that requires you to tweak your answer, put a large noticeable circle around the modifier in the question and draw an asterisk in the location your final answer will need to go. This way, you will be reminded of it both when you put down your answer and when you are double-checking the question later.

Your teacher may allow you to choose the questions on your test. For instance, he may say to answer fifteen of twenty questions. If you are given this option, choose to answer those questions that you are confident you can answer correctly. Do not do the remaining questions unless your teacher specifically says these answers will count as extra credit or can replace incorrect answers. Otherwise, doing so will only waste your time and possibly cause your teacher to grade different questions than those you would have preferred. If your teacher does not make it clear what he will do with extra answers, ask him; it is important. If he is willing to give credit in some way, still only answer the remaining questions after fully and correctly completing the required questions. If you end up not having time to do any extras, that is fine. Your high grade will come from doing what was required of you.

Test questions are generally formatted as free response, matching, short answer, fill in the blank, or multiple choice questions. You want to be prepared for and comfortable with whatever selections your teacher might make. Let's take a look at each of these question types and how to handle them.

    o   **Responding to Free Response and Essay Questions**

When it comes to free response answers, appearances matter. The way your answer looks impacts your teacher's impression of it, and, consequently, it can affect your grade. Make an effort to write neatly and to write darkly enough so that the text is easily legible. If you need to cross something out, keep it tidy by drawing a single line through the word or words (~~mistake~~) rather than scribbling a large blob over the offending content. If you choose to erase the text instead, rub your eraser lightly over the paper so as to avoid causing smudges or rips in the page. If you press too hard you may permanently smudge your test paper. Some students prefer to use whiteout, but this takes up time and can be messy and smelly. I recommend you stick with the quicker methods of slashing and erasing.

Another way to keep your essay neat is by spacing the text. If you skip lines in your essay, you will have room to come back and fill in more information later if need be. If you have found that you frequently end up coming back to your essays to write more, this technique may be for you. Leave regular spaces between every line. And, if you decide while writing your essay that you will come back to one particular section later, leave several consecutive blank lines in the appropriate area.

It is important to maintain continuity while writing your essay. If at any point while writing your essay you think of the answer to or an idea for a previous problem, jot your thoughts in the margin and continue working on your essay. Otherwise, you will put yourself out of the appropriate frame of mind and may lose track of what you were planning to say in your essay.

Finally, we come to the free response guidelines. When you take your test, you will have the necessary knowledge to answer the free response questions. It comes down to making sure you write all of the information in the correct format. The following guidelines will help you with this part. Memorize and follow these simple steps.

General Free Response Guidelines (BORP)

1. **Brainstorm.** Brainstorming is the most important part of the process as far as content goes, so let your mind relax and fill with ideas to use for your answer.

Write down all relevant facts that come to your mind in response to the question. If you are unsure if something should be included or not, write it. List all of your ideas on a piece of scrap paper or on the back of the test page. This is your chance to quickly jot down all possibly relevant information; no sorting, ordering, or selecting of any type is involved. If you are low on time, try doing the majority of your brainstorming mentally so that you still have some time to create an outline (see step #2).

2. **Outline.** Also on a scrap piece of paper, sketch an outline for your essay. Generally, free response questions take the standard 5-paragraph format: introduction, point #1, point #2, point #3, conclusion. Each point requires several supporting facts. In order to follow this format, select the relevant information from your brainstorming list and order your outline accordingly. Outlines let you preview your essay ahead of time and help you to organize your ideas in a logical and intelligent format.

3. **Respond.** Next you need to put your plan into action. Your first paragraph should introduce the subject in question and provide a succinct answer or thesis in response to the question posed. Your next paragraph should explain point #1. Your point is an important piece of supporting information justifying why you chose the answer that you did in the introduction. Each point should be backed up with examples, facts, information from class discussions, statistics, quotes, etc. In general, give your strongest point first to start your response out with a bang. End with a strong concluding paragraph that summarizes your points and reinforces how they support your answer. Keep in mind that each sentence you

write should make a point that helps to answer the question. Take advantage of the fact that your points are linked to one another by your thesis, and make the transitions between them smooth. If you can include any new course vocabulary in your essay, it would be a nice touch.

4. **Proofread.** Finally, it is time for you to proofread your essay. Look for any errors in grammar, spelling, sentence structure, or logic, and make sure your handwriting is legible. Avoid any casual abbreviations that you are accustomed to using, such as the symbol @ (at) or the letter *u* (you) in place of the proper words. I have seen such mistakes slip into formal assignments of students of all ages.

Remember, free response questions allow for partial credit and are often based more on what you say correctly than what you state incorrectly. For this reason, even if you are unsure about the correct answer, get down as much information as you can. The process alone of writing out your thoughts may help you to come up with the proper answer.

o **Responding to Multiple Choice Questions**

Multiple choice questions are best answered systematically. First and foremost, make sure to check the directions just in case you are allowed to give more than one answer for a question. Then, read the first question while avoiding looking at the answer choices. Often, answer choices are designed to throw you off track, to *seem* correct or to plant a wrong idea seed in your head. They may cause you to answer another question than the one being asked, or they may cloud your initial understanding of the question. Therefore, after reading the question, take a moment to determine the correct answer in your own words. By knowing your answer first, you avoid these pitfalls.

Once you have the correct answer in mind, go ahead and look at the answer choices. In order to select the correct choice, start at the first answer and decide whether or not it corresponds with your idea. If it does not match with your thoughts, then you should slash that letter option out. Move on to the next answer choice and do the same. When you find the correct answer, circle it. Even if you select the very first answer, finish reading and crossing out all other choices, just in case there is a better option available. Note that often multiple choice directions ask you to choose the answer that *best* satisfies each question. This means that sometimes more than one answer choice can correctly answer the question, but one does so better than the rest.

By following the above method, you physically reinforce the idea that you should be able to justify why your answer choice is the correct one. For each answer choice, you make a deliberate decision to circle it or to slash it out. As was mentioned in **Responding to Free Response and Essay Questions**, sometimes it can help to write out your answer. If either none or more than one of the selections seem appropriate, write down on scrap paper what you think the correct answer should be. Also, write each viable answer choice over again in your own words. Getting the information on paper will help you to better see which answer choice corresponds best to your thoughts and will help you to make the correct selection.

If you are given a separate answer sheet on which to put your answers, make sure to still write your answers on the actual test. That way you can later double-check that you filled in the answer sheet correctly. You don't want to lose points for accidentally filling out the answer sheet incorrectly. If you are using a Scantron answer sheet (a separate form requiring you to fill in bubbles) and decide to skip a multiple choice problem, be careful. As I mentioned earlier, with only one exception you should always give at least your best guess, rather than leave the question blank, before moving on. If you do skip a problem for some reason, make sure to skip that row on your Scantron as well. Students have ruined their test scores, both in class and on the SAT and other standardized tests, by accidentally filling in their answers in the wrong row. Do not let this happen to you. If you skip a question, immediately draw a light pencil line through that number and row of bubbled letters on the Scantron. That way, when you go to fill in the answer to the next problem, you will not fill in the preceding number by mistake. When you come back to the skipped question later, be sure to erase the pencil line in its entirety before filling in your answer. Otherwise, the machine that grades the Scantron sheet may have difficulty reading your answer and thus mark the question as incorrect even when it is not.

Compared to most other forms of questioning, multiple choice sections give you a good shot at guessing the correct answer. This is because the correct answer is directly in front of you. All you have to do is pick it out. If, after reading a multiple choice question, you realize that you have no idea what the answer is, immediately look at the answer choices. Cross out any answers that you know are incorrect. From the remaining questions, make an educated guess as to which one is correct. Make sure to leave a question mark by this problem so that you can spend more time on it later. You may have a sudden flash of brainpower while working on another problem and think of the correct answer for this one.

A final point on multiple choice questions is that certain answer choices tend to be wrong.

- If two answer choices are exact opposites, it is likely that one of them is a wrong answer choice and that the other is the correct response.
- Extreme answer choices—which imply that *only* this method is true or that this specific occurrence *always* takes place—tend to be wrong.

While the subject matter has a great impact on possible answer choices, these tips can help guide you in the right direction.

- **Responding to Fill in the Blank Questions**

    Your fill in the blank section may or may not include a word bank, and your word bank can vary in its usefulness. Sometimes you are allowed to use words more than once or there can be extra words in the word bank, both of which are not quite as helpful as having a word bank in which all words must be used only once. Just as with multiple choice questions, read the fill in the blank question and then try to think of the answer without looking at the word bank, if there is one. Then, find the word bank choice that best matches your answer and fill it in the blank. Check off the answer in the word bank. Even if you are allowed to use a word more than once, it can be helpful to know how many times you have used each one. If you use a specific word in the word bank a second time, put a second check by it.

    If you cannot figure out the answer for a particular blank, it often helps to skip it and come back to it later. If you have a one-time-use word bank, you may be able to narrow down your options some. Even if you don't have a word bank, you may gain a better understanding of what your teacher is looking for as you go.

There are also some other tricks you can use to solve tough fill in the blank problems.

- For one, a blank often will require a specific type of word, such as a plural verb, a word that starts with a vowel, or a singular noun. Look through the word bank for those few words that fulfill the specific requirement and put small circles (°) next to them. Then, consider the content of the marked words and decide on the best one. Before you do this, check the directions. Sometimes you will be told that you can change the form or tense of the word bank words, and thus this particular method could not be used to help narrow your choices. Once you have answered the question for which you made the small circles next to the answer choices, erase the small circles so that you will be able to repeat the same method again for another problem.

- Another option is to try placing each available word bank choice into the blank and then to consider if it makes sense. Once again, put a small circle next to any word of which you approve. Then compare the marked words and decide which one is most likely to be the correct answer.

Fill in the blank questions with word banks often seem like overgrown multiple choice problems. Use any clues you can to your advantage. The correct response is limited by key words in the question, word bank options, grammatical requirements, and content scope.

- **Responding to Short Answer Questions**

  These questions are similar to free response questions in that you have to write out an answer that you think of entirely on your own. However, keep your short answer short. Look at the directions or ask your teacher, if necessary, to find out if he wants you to restate the question in your answer and/or to write in complete sentences. Sometimes, teachers prefer you simply to write the answer, even if it is only one word.

  Typically, there are several specific principles that apply to short answer questions.

- Restating the question will not give you any points and will only waste time.

- You should write in complete, concise, grammatically correct sentences.

- As with other question types, you should make sure to fully answer the question being asked and not assume the grader knows anything that you do not say.

Restate the question only if you are specifically required to do so. In **When You Don't Know**, we will go over how you should answer short answer questions to which you do not know the answer.

     o   **Responding to Matching Questions**

        Matching sections are similar to fill in the blank and multiple choice questions. As with these others, before you begin, you need to read the directions and make sure that each response can only be used once. If this is the case, then check off each answer after you have used it once; you then know that it is not in the running to be an answer for the following questions. If using an answer for one match does not mean you cannot use it for another, check it off anyway; only now your checks will be used as a tally of how many times you have used a specific response.

        Whenever you have trouble figuring out the answer to a matching problem, look at each response that you have not yet crossed off and try matching it with the question. You will probably find it helpful to skip that particular problem and come back to it after completing the other problems in the match section, as this will usually narrow down your choices. For the problem in question, put small circles by those remaining matches you think could be correct. When you have narrowed it down to a few options, make an educated guess as to which one of these is the most likely answer.

     ❖ **Spotting Tricks**

        Trick questions can mean the downfall of even the most knowledgeable student, but that doesn't have to be the case. A sharp eye and understanding common trick question set-ups will keep you away from the tricks and in with the treats. Take a close look at the question's wording to make sure you answer it properly. The following pages describe the four main traps for which you should be on the lookout.

1. **Opposites.** This is a fairly common and unnecessary error. Test questions often include words that negate their entire meaning. If an inattentive student misses that, he will get the question wrong, no matter how hard he studied. When you see a word that alters what the question is asking for, circle it immediately. These include words such as *never, except, but, not,* and *excluding.* Especially on multiple choice questions, students often forget the specifics of the question while reading through the answer choices, and then they fall for a wrong answer choice. For this reason, among others, you should always think of the answer to a multiple choice question before you look to select an answer choice.

2. **Units.** When dealing with mathematics and the sciences, units are often a required part of the answer. Make sure your units are written as specified. For example, the problem may give you background information in pounds, but then ask you to give your answer in kilograms. In such cases, when you first read the question, circle the part of the question that calls for the specific unit type and draw an asterisk in the area where your final response is to go. When you go to write down your answer, your eyes will be drawn to the circled information and the asterisk, and you will be sure to convert your answer accordingly. Another variation of this trick set-up can be seen in multiple choice style questions. Although the question may not directly ask you to change units, the answer choices will have different units than those you used to calculate the answer. For instance, your answer may be *50 pounds*, but the answer choices will all be written in terms of kilograms. And you can be sure that one of the answer choices will be the same value as yours but have different units, in this case such a choice would be *50 kilograms*, so that the unscrupulous student will quickly pick this wrong answer choice and move on. In fact, the correct value, *22.7 kilograms*, is a very different answer choice and would not be selected unless the student was paying careful attention to the units of the problem and answers. When it comes down to units, always check to make sure the units in the answer match those for which the question calls. Likewise, sometimes, such as in physics, the test question may include units that do not work in the normally applicable equation. In such instances, you will have to convert the given units into their proper form

before applying the equation.

3. **Extras.** In subjects such as math, the test makers know how you will set out to solve a given problem. They will take advantage of this and throw in tricky little *extras* that you otherwise would not expect. They will require you to modify the way in which you reach your answer, thus altering your usual routine for solving the problem. If you forget to alter your solution, you will end up with the incorrect answer. For example, as was previously mentioned, you may be used to solving for the value of a single variable, such as that *one* vanilla-frosted strawberry cupcake. The test makers, knowing this, will ask you to solve for the price of *three* cupcakes. They are counting on you to forget while working out the problem that you must multiply your end result by three. If you notice that a question asks for something you will not be solving for directly, such as the three cupcakes rather than the one, circle that part of the question. This way, when you double check the question, you will notice the stipulation and make sure to check your answer for accuracy. Furthermore, immediately after reading the question, write the condition in the area in which you will be putting your answer. In the case of the cupcakes, on the line meant for your final answer of the total cost, you can write a *3* with your pencil. Then, when you go to record your answer after working through the math, you will have to erase the *3* and will be reminded to convert your answer to the cost of three cupcakes.

4. **Simplicity.** Sometimes you may breeze over a super easy question. However, be careful if you encounter one of these freebies, just in case they are more difficult than they at first seem. While it is often true that your teacher will give you a freebie question, he or she is not always going to be so nice. That really easy question may include one of the tricks we discussed above or may require more in-depth thought. Either way, when you come to a noticeably easy question, give it a second look to make sure it is as easy as it really seems. Students often complain of getting the easy questions wrong. Give these questions adequate time, analysis, and thought to ensure you get the high score you deserve.

❖ **When You Don't Know**

Even with your excellent preparation, it may happen that you come across a test question that baffles you or that you suddenly find yourself short on time and unable to give a question the thought it demands. If either scenario occurs, don't panic! It happens to everyone. By keeping calm, you will continue performing at your test best. We have already discussed how to narrow down your options when confronted with multiple choice, fill in the blank, or matching type questions. In this section, we will continue this focus with a special emphasis on how to compose answers to short answer and essay type questions to which you do not know the answer.

The first point to remember is that generally the grading system will only add points and not subtract points for even the most unconventional response. Therefore, there is no reason not to answer every single question on your test, even if some of your answers are complete guesses. Furthermore, you have dedicated hours of your time to studying this material. You know the answer in some form or other, and you want to use that to your advantage.

If you have some vague idea as to what the correct answer should be—and you generally will—take out a piece of scrap paper and quickly brainstorm and write all the relevant information you can about your best guess for the answer. As I mentioned before, writing your thoughts can really get the cogs turning in your head. Also, seeing the information on paper may stimulate your mind to come up with the appropriate answer. For a short answer question, select your answer from the information you jotted down and from the new insights you gained in the process. If you are dealing with an essay question, use this information to create a reasonable thesis and supporting outline. Sometimes, even if a question does not call for a written response, such as a multiple choice question, it will still help you to jot down any relevant information you can think of. Doing so will help you to eliminate answers that must be incorrect and will help you to identify the actual correct response.

For certain questions requiring written responses, you may be able to get points by explaining how you would answer the question if you could, or by making and supporting a good prediction of the answer even though you are having trouble solving the problem through conventional methods. In a math problem, for instance, your teacher may ask you to solve for the surface area of a circle drawn onto graph paper. Maybe you don't remember the equation you learned in math class, but you can count the little square grids inside the object and estimate the surface area from that. In another scenario, you may know how to do the problem but not have the necessary information to do it. Once, on a chemistry test I took, the first half of a problem asked me to solve for the chemical formula of a compound and the second part asked me to use that answer to determine the molar mass of that compound. I couldn't get the correct answer to the first part of the question (it turns out it was a simple *units* mistake on my part—see **Spotting Tricks**), but I knew how to solve for the second part of the question. Teachers give us tests to see if we really understand the material, and I did; I had to show my teacher that. Since I didn't have the proper chemical formula to calculate the molar mass, I made one up and wrote a side note to my teacher explaining why I was using my own chemical formula. This allowed me to get some credit for the second part of the problem. My friend who had also not been able to figure out the chemical formula, also thanks to an oversight on that tricky units conversion step, got both parts of the question wrong and received no credit whatsoever. Your teacher is looking to see if you are capable of getting the answer, so do your best to show him that you can.

There are several ways to handle a problem when you are either out of time or have absolutely no idea as to what the answer should be. Remember never to leave a question blank.

1. Tests often present new information and then expect you to answer questions by taking the new concepts into consideration. Look at any information with which the test provides you, including ideas that were directly given, such as specific formulas, and those indirectly given, such as ideas integrated into other questions. Try to identify any common elements between the test question and the presented information. Maybe the question is based on similar concepts and you have yet to draw the connection. Also, reevaluate your interpretation of the question. It may be asking something different than you originally thought. Keep your mind relaxed and let the ideas flow. Students often get their tests back only to find that questions they thought were impossible were in fact basic questions grounded in other ideas presented on the test.

2. If you cannot make a connection between the test content and the question, look for any relationship between the question and what you already know. Try relaxing your mind and thinking about when you heard the concept in question discussed at any point in the past. Search your memory for small clues; maybe you remember reading about the topic in your textbook, taking notes on it, hearing one of your peers ask your teacher about it. Who said it? Where were you? When was it? What did your surroundings look like? Imagine yourself back in that situation and then focus on identifying anything that may help you to answer the question. The answer may suddenly come to you in a flash, or you may gradually gain a vague recollection of ideas. Through the bits and pieces of what you remember, create an intelligent response.

3. Sometimes it will help to remove yourself from the situation. Try stepping back for a moment and looking at the big picture. Pretend this was not a test you were taking, but simply a question you were posed by another person. Without forcing yourself to concentrate on information you have learned in class, create your own logical response. Use your common sense and reasoning abilities to think of a sensible answer, even if it only depends on information you already knew outside of class.

4. If you are familiar with a topic closely related to the one about which the question is asking, it may help you to focus on that. Think about what you know of this topic and look for any connections you can draw. Likewise, during an essay test, you may decide to write some about this closely related subject if you have nothing to write on the specific question being asked. This may help you to come up with correct answer or at least to earn some partial credit from your teacher.

5. If you really have no clue about what the answer is, you can start listing off what it is not. You can jot your thoughts down to help you come up with the correct answer. If you are answering a question that calls for a written response, you might as well let your teacher in on your thoughts. Tell him on paper what you

know the answer isn't; that in and of itself can show that you have some idea as to what the correct answer is.

6. If all else fails, just give your best guess, or any guess for that matter. If you are out of time and have a few multiple choice questions left, it is better to fill in random answers than to leave them totally blank. If you need to respond to a free response question in that short time, leave it as a quick outline with all the facts you can include. Show that you know the information even if you don't have enough time to make it read nicely. Write *OUT OF TIME* somewhere near your response so that your teacher knows that you would have been able to polish your answer better if you had had the time. If you need more time, then don't hand in your test until your teacher absolutely insists on it. Sometimes your teacher will give you extra time without announcing it. Just stay where you are and keep working as efficiently as you can. Do not hand in your test until you have double- and triple-checked it or your teacher makes you. You may choose to ask for more time as well, as will be discussed in **Asking for Extras**.

❖ **Asking for Extras**

There are a couple main *extras* for which you may at some point have to ask your teacher, those being time and credit. If you are asking for a favor that will only be applicable to you, try your best to ask out of the hearing range of other students. While your teacher may feel it is appropriate to grant you your request, he may feel uncomfortable saying so in front of others if he would prefer not to extend the opportunity to all members of the class. Ask for these favors quietly, respectfully, and only when needed.

If you find that you are out of time for a test but still have a lot to go, you will need to bring this up with your teacher. If he or she doesn't say anything but allows you to continue working, then that's great. Don't stop; and continue to work as quickly as you can. If, however, you have to go somewhere, such as to your next class, or if your teacher insists that you hand in the test, then you need to ask for more time. Tell your teacher the truth: that you have been working as quickly as you can but that you still need more time to get to the rest of the questions. If there is not time for you to work more on your test at the moment, either due to your teacher's time restraints or yours, provide another time at which you will be able to return to complete the test. If that is not good for your teacher, then ask when would be best for him. Remember that you will need to complete the test as soon as possible so that your teacher can grade and return the exams in a timely manner. This is one of the many times at which your teacher's decision will impact your grade, and this is therefore one of the many reasons why you should adhere to the guidance in **Talking with Your Teacher**, because your teacher's impressions of you can sway his decision one way or the other. Still, understand that although it would be nice of your teacher to grant you more time, and although he may *want to do it*, there may be other factors that will demand he says no. For instance, he may feel that it is unfair to the other students in the class to let you have extra time. If you need the extra time, make sure to ask for it, even if you think your teacher will say no.

In the unlikely event that you do not get a good score on your test, you can ask your teacher for an extra credit assignment. Tell your teacher that you feel that your work on the test and the grade you received are not reflective of the tremendous amount of studying you did and of the knowledge you have of the test material. Ask your teacher for some extra credit work to give you the opportunity to show what you have learned and to improve your grade. Teachers vary in their willingness to give extra credit opportunities. Some teachers never allow extra credit while many others will gladly let you retake an entire test or do a special project. Asking for extra credit is always worth a try. When you are behaving as you should in class and doing your work, your teacher takes note. He or she also may feel that you should have a chance to improve your grade. As a rule, whenever your teacher offers the opportunity for extra credit, make sure to do it.

When You Get the Test Back

Considering that you have been following the guidelines and techniques in this book, you are bound to do well on your test. You may still get a couple of problems wrong, though, and when you do, you want to make use of it. Learning from one's mistakes is the mark of a wise individual. You can use your incorrect answers to improve your academic work and your study habits for the future. Most students get their test back, look at their grade, and then stuff the paper into their binders. As a successful student, you need to play this situation differently. You will analyze your graded test to ensure that your teacher graded it correctly and then will use it to enhance your studying techniques for the future.

The first thing to do when you get your test back is to look at your grade. Even if you feel apprehensive about it, waiting won't change anything. Furthermore, by reviewing your test as soon as you get it back, you can check that it was graded correctly while your teacher is still around. Quickly look through the test and find any questions for which points were taken off. Make sure that the correct amount of points was taken off and that you have at least a rudimentary understanding as to why they were taken off. If you do not understand, ask your teacher for clarification immediately because the deduction may have been a mistake. Also, check your teacher's math. Teachers often make mathematical errors on test grades. Make sure that the correct amount of points was taken off. If too many points were deducted, let your teacher know so that he can recalculate and then record your new higher grade.

Once you are sure you have the correct grade, it is time to further analyze any errors you may have made. You will probably want to do this at home where you will have more time to review the material. Add *review test* to your homework planner under the appropriate course heading. If your teacher does not allow students to take graded exams home, and you do not have enough time to fully review your test in class, ask your teacher if you can come in another time to go over your exam. When you review your test, look at each item you got wrong and think about what caused you to give an incorrect answer. It may have been a mistake due to failing to spot a trick question, a result of misunderstanding the directions, a careless error, such as knowing the right answer but writing it incorrectly, or maybe you simply did not know the information the question called for because you did not study it well enough. Read over your teacher's comments to gain further insight into any ways in which you can improve your study and test-taking techniques.

For each of your classes, keep a running tally of the reasons why points were deducted from your tests and quizzes. Students often find that a specific type of error, such as failure to convert to proper units, is responsible for the majority of their missed points. This way you will be able to focus on and actively avoid making this mistake on future exams in the course. If your problem was a lack of content knowledge, analyze how and why you missed that particular information in your studying. Was it something you didn't have in your notes, forgot to read in your textbook, or missed when you were absent from class? Recognize where things went wrong, and keep a sharp eye out to avoid a future recurrence.

Finally, your test gives you insight into what future tests will be like in that class. Take a moment to analyze the test questions. Are they similar to questions used in your textbook or to ones that your teacher brought up in class and assigned for homework? Teachers often use specific materials as a basis for making up test questions. See if you can identify what sources your teacher may have modeled his or her test after, or at least what materials have questions similar in type and content to those of your test. When the next test rolls around, you will have these sources and this exam as part of your artillery for answering test-predicting question #2. When you are finished, file this exam in your at-home binder in the section for this particular class.

After identifying any problems in your preparation for and taking of this test, take a moment to consider how your preparation went overall. Were you more or less prepared than you needed to be for the test? Were there additional items that would have been helpful to study? Does this teacher focus his tests more on the larger picture or on smaller details? You can often answer these questions right after taking the test. Bearing in mind the answers to these questions, consider any other ways in which you may be able to improve your study habits in the future, especially for this particular course.

Stress Reducers

Most students feel stress at some point. Some get this stress more often than others and some get it to a greater degree of severity than others. Since you will be keeping on top of your work and studying your material daily, you are much less prone to the severe cases of stress that come with last-minute cramming and information overload. Still there may be times when you feel stress, but don't allow the feeling to overwhelm or control you. Stress can come in the form of a headache, mood swings, tense muscles, insomnia, loss of focus or in other ways. But no worries; there are plenty of ways to combat stress. Let's go over some simple ideas you can incorporate into your everyday life in order to reduce and diminish any stress you may be experiencing and to free yourself of its deleterious effects.

If you feel anxious while you are studying for your test, use the optimum-rest method described below.

Optimum-rest Method

1. Dim the lights in the room if you can, and lie on your back with your knees raised, your feet resting flat on the floor, and your head and neck muscles relaxed.

2. Separate your feet so that they are shoulder width apart, and point your toes in and your heals out, allowing your knees to fall together.

3. Cross your arms over your chest and allow your hands to hang limply along your neck.

4. Close your eyes, clear your thoughts, and imagine a peaceful and quiet surrounding, such as an empty beach with the waves crashing gently.

> *You can control your mind and body through your breathing. Stressed people take short shallow breaths. To relax, take long deep breaths through your nose.*
>
> *Some experts claim that almost 97% of Americans don't breathe "correctly." In order to be included among that lucky 3%, take deep, full breaths that cause your abdomen to expand. Your shoulders should not need to rise as they do during superficial breathing.*

If you are at a place where you cannot lie down, such as in the library studying or in your seat waiting for an exam to begin, try the palming method.

Palming Method

1. Block all light from your eyes by gently covering them with the palm of your hands. To avoid pressing on or putting any pressure on your eyes, place the lower part of your palms on your cheekbones and place your fingers on your forehead.

2. Your eyes are blanketed in darkness, but remain open. Imagine and visualize a pleasant scene, and move your eyes to look more closely at different parts of the scene. Avoid keeping your eyes on one spot; in this method it is important that you move your eyes. For instance, if you picture a serene meadow, first look at the puffy clouds in the blue sky, then at the overgrown green grass; move your

eyes to a yellow dandelion, then to a doe grazing peacefully. Allow your eyes to wander.

3.   You should feel relaxed again in less than a minute.

You can use the count-of-three method to calm and focus yourself during an exam.

Count-of-Three Method

1.   Inhale slowly through your nose while silently counting to three.

2.   Hold your breath for another count of three.

3.   Silently count to three as you exhale through your nose.

4.   Pause and count to three once again; then repeat steps one through four several times. Once you have the timing and pauses down, you can continue without counting each number.

> *It may be that the stress we feel today was actually biologically meant for something else many thousands of years ago. It is thought that our ancestors felt stress in response to physical conditions, such as would be the case in a fight with a wild dog. Early man's response would be physical as well. Today, it is not a wild dog but a chemistry test that stresses most students. Yet, biologically, we are of a similar build, meaning we can still release stress by means of physical exertion.*

Exercise is another healthy and effective way to reduce stress. Exercise has also been shown to improve memory and mental function. Physical activity exercises the heart, which allows more oxygen to get to all parts of your body—including your brain. As far as stress goes, exercise gives you an outlet. You can take a brisk walk, go jogging, do an exercise video, lift weights or knock around a punching bag. After vigorous activity, most people are able to think more clearly with less distracting thoughts whizzing around their minds and are better able to focus their energy. For many people, exercise makes them feel better in a general sense. Research studies have found that exercise results in increased levels of serotonin, a chemical that makes people feel happy and less anxious. As exercise psychologist Andrea Dunn, Ph.D., of The Cooper Institute in Dallas, says of exercise, "It affects the biology in the brain in the same way that anti-depressant drugs do." Try out some exercise, no matter what condition you are in. It doesn't have to be strenuous, just something that gets your body moving and heart rate up so that you have an outlet for your stress and are not left sitting there dwelling over anxious thoughts.

You may also want to join a club at school, such as the chess or dance club, so that you have a source of fun outside your normal routine. Or, you can set aside a couple of hours to enjoy yourself every week. Plan a precise time in the near future to go see a movie, and whenever you feel stressed think about how you are going to soon enjoy seeing that movie. You may want to go and get a professional massage to help chill you out. Sometimes, a simple chat with a friend, sibling, or your mom or dad may be enough. If you feel particularly stressed, consider going to a guidance counselor for help relieving your anxiety. If there is a specific problem that has been bothering you, bringing it up to someone else may shed new light on any possible solutions.

As some final advice on reducing stress, realize that you are in charge of the thoughts in your mind. Don't let them negatively affect your studies and general functioning. Maintain a calm and relaxed attitude as you prepare for and take your tests, and don't stress the small stuff. If you can't decide on some little issue that doesn't really have much importance, then just choose whatever is easiest for you; flip a coin if need be. Be flexible, and enjoy life. ☺

Summary: Test Time

- Start studying for your tests well ahead of time.

- Answer the four predicting questions included in **What to Expect**. Put your answers to use with the guidance in **What to Review**.

- Avoid study groups unless you tailor them specifically to your needs.

- One of the most important characteristics of a successful student is the ability to study efficiently. Choose an appropriate study technique from **How**. Techniques include: examples, acronyms, sentences, alphabetizing, relations, size, pictures, path, self-quiz, repetition, recording, review sheet, flashcards, implications, equations, song, poetry, visualization, color, teaching, and assorted variations of these techniques.

- The night before the exam, prepare everything you will need with you during the test, including a pencil or erasable pen. Make sure to wear comfortable clothing.

- Always double-check each of your answers before handing in your test.

- Each question type (essay, multiple choice, fill in the blank, short answer, and matching) should be dealt with using the skills set specified.

- Keep an eye out for the four basic trick question types: opposites, units, extras, and simplicity.

- Never leave a question blank unless there is a guessing penalty. If you find yourself stuck on a question, try the strategies described in **When You Don't Know**.

- Ask for extra time or credit if you need it. It is important to treat your teacher respectfully even if he responds in the negative.

- When you get your test back, make sure that your grade is accurate and set a time to further review the material. Identify any improvements you can make in your test preparation and adapt your study methods accordingly.

- Follow the ideas in **Stress Reducers** to keep your mind and body healthy

- If your routine makes you feel depressed or stressed, try altering it. Join a school club, see a movie, get a massage—do something fun!

7. Doing Reports

In this chapter, we will discuss the final element of your success: how to create great written reports and oral presentations. We will go over every key step of the process, including how to go about doing research. You have come this far, let's have a strong finish!

Choosing a Topic

Sometimes your teacher will assign you a specific topic for your paper, while other times he will leave the choice to you. When the choice is yours, you have the opportunity to conform the assignment to your specific interests and talents to make the project both easier and more enjoyable for yourself.

Keep your main goal in mind; you want to get a top grade on this assignment. Choose a topic that will enable you to do so. Students often pick a topic they think sounds cool, but then they have difficulty creating a solid report. At this stage, your first considerations should include the relative ease of availability of information on this topic and your familiarity with the subject matter. You want to select a topic you feel comfortable working with and about which you can find ample information. Take out a piece of paper and list all potential topics that you believe fulfill these criteria. Use the tips below to help you think of appropriate ideas. Later, you will select the topic you are most interested in learning more and writing about.

- A subject that was discussed in depth during class can be a great choice of topic. You may have to narrow it down some, but either way it works as a great starting point. Look through your notes to review subjects that were brought up in class. They are concepts you are familiar with and on which you already have some information.

- Conduct a simple internet search on some of the broader topics from which you have to choose. Look for any material for which there is a particularly abundant amount of information available. This way you know you will be choosing a topic that is not difficult to research.

- Other good sources for topics include your textbook, supplementary readings, and class handouts.

- Ask your teacher for topic suggestions.

- Spend some time brainstorming ideas. Set the timer for a specific amount of time, say five minutes, to think of ideas. Sit down with a pen and notepad and, for the full amount of time, write down any and all ideas that come to your mind. It doesn't matter if you think an idea is too broad, too farfetched, or too anything else. One unlikely topic you come up with while brainstorming may be the catalyst for an excellent idea later on. Keep writing *any* ideas that come to your mind. You want to have a long list of topics from which to choose once you are done brainstorming.

From the ideas you listed, pick the best topic. Make sure it is a concept you are comfortable working with, for which there is a good amount of published information, and that you will enjoy learning more about.

If you are working on a persuasive paper and do not already feel strongly in support of a certain position, you will need to conduct preliminary research in order to choose which side of the debate you will defend and which side you will rebut. There needs to be a good supply of readily available information to support your position. Many students start by taking one position on a project and end up changing their point of view by the end of their research. This can squander a lot of time and effort. You do not want to go through that, so before choosing your slant on a topic, look through some of the relevant information and see what side you can most easily and most strongly defend and support.

As soon as you can, tell your teacher your topic to make sure that he or she finds it acceptable. Your teacher may want to adjust your idea some by narrowing or broadening the topic. By clearing your topic with your teacher before you put a great deal of time into the project, you ensure that you do not waste time doing work that will later be irrelevant. You want to work on a topic that you know your teacher approves of and to which he will be willing to give a good grade.

Researching

Before you delve into the research process, you need to brainstorm once more. This time, you already know your topic. Now you need to define your research interests. For this brainstorm session, list any questions you want your research to answer or any points you want to be able to raise in your project. From your list, you will select reasonable subtopics that will be important in supporting your thesis (see page 159). Try to keep your subtopic titles as concise as possible. Once you know and have written down the particular subjects you want to research, you will be able to use your time efficiently to find exactly what you need to know. During the course of your research, you may identify other important subtopics to include, or you may learn that one of your original subtopics is actually unimportant. Be flexible about adding, substituting, or deleting subtopics as needed. Maintain a list, no matter how dynamic it may be, of all of your subtopics.

Your teacher may set standards concerning what type of materials you are allowed to use as references in your assignment. Many teachers do not allow students to use websites and certain other materials as sources of reliable information. Make sure you follow any standards your teacher sets. You can also ask your teacher if he or she has any specific ideas for sources related to your particular topic. For instance, your teacher may know of a certain book, periodical, or encyclopedia that includes a special section on your topic of interest.

Print out or photocopy any of the relevant information you find. Read through it, carefully looking for your specific subtopics and any other interesting information. When you find something relevant, highlight it. In the margin, jot down the specific subtopic to which the highlighted information relates. Doing this is vital to the organization and integrity of your paper.

> *Your local library may have great resources, so make sure to check it out in addition to your school library. Also, many public libraries have access to useful online databases that will allow you to find many peer-reviewed journals and scholarly publications that you cannot access with a Google search. These are excellent reliable sources for research papers. Call or visit your local library for more detailed information, and make sure to go ahead and get a library card if you do not already have one.*

Once you have completed highlighting and selecting your information, you are ready for the next step. In general, for papers at least four to five pages or more, you will need to make note cards, as we are about to discuss. For a shorter research paper, you may be able to skip this step and go directly to making your outline. Before continuing on however, make sure to consider whether your shorter paper could in fact benefit from note cards. Note cards are very helpful in that they allow you to easily organize and consider all of the information that you plan to include in your assignment, and thus they enable you to write an intelligent, structured, and well-designed paper. Obtain a set of note cards, preferably the 3" x 5" size, and carry out the following steps.

How to Make Useful Note Cards

1. Assign a number to each source that you have used and highlighted. For example, if you are doing a report on the benefits of stem cell research and use an article from a specific scientific journal, write #1 very large on that article. If you also used a book on stem cell research, then consider that book source #2. Write the number on each photocopied source so that it is visible, and list the titles and their corresponding numbers on a separate sheet of paper as well. It is not important which source you give which number, as long as you assign every source a number.

2. Consider your highlights in order, beginning with source #1. For your first highlight in the source, decide if the highlighted information is important for your research paper; if not, disregard the highlight and move on to the next one. If you decide you want to use a highlight, write the important information it presents down on one of your note cards. Each note card should contain the information from *one* highlight only. You will probably make many note cards, depending on the depth and breadth of your project. Write the information succinctly and try to use only one side of the card.

3. After adding a piece of highlighted information to a note card, immediately write in the top right corner the source number and specific page from which the information came. This allows for easy reference in case you need to look up the information again, either during the course of writing the paper or to create a works cited page.

4. In the top left-hand corner of the note card, write the subtopic to which the information on the card pertains. If multiple subtopics are applicable, include the others as well. You can decide later to which subtopic the information better applies.

Your Thesis

Your thesis is the main point you are trying to make with your paper. If you are writing a persuasive paper, your thesis makes a strong statement of your side of the argument. If your paper is informative, it should state an insightful and edifying point based on your ideas and research, such as *William Shakespeare's play* <u>*The Tempest*</u> *is really about colonial imperialism.* Your thesis generally should not include detailed supporting information. It is simply a position you state at the end of your introduction, usually as the last sentence of the first paragraph. There will be plenty of time to support your thesis later on in your paper.

Organization

Organization is key to having a great paper. You have already gathered all of your information; you know your thesis and all of your supporting subtopics and their details. Creating an outline enables you to sort out the information for yourself so that it will be easier for you to present it in a logical order. Both you and your reader will benefit from the clarity and understanding that go hand in hand with having an effective outline.

As a precursor to your outline, take a second look at the sheet of paper on which you listed all of your subtopics. Decide on the order in which they would be most logically presented in order to support your thesis. If there is a chronological difference between the subtopics, you may want to arrange them in order of date or time. If the subtopics differ in complexity, you should probably start with the least complicated subtopic before building up to the more advanced ones. After choosing the appropriate general order of your topics, it is time to make your outline.

First, take out a piece of paper and write the subtopics in your selected order. Leave five to ten empty lines between each listed topic or type your outline on the computer. Take out your note cards and divide them into piles by subtopic, as listed in the cards' top left corners. Then, go through all of the cards in the category of your first subtopic, and put them in the order you feel most appropriate for your paper. The nice thing about note cards is that they allow you room for play; nothing is set in stone. You can throw a couple out, make the middle card the last one, or make the last one first.

Keep playing around with the order until you know you have the order in which you want to present the information for that particular subtopic. Read through the cards in the order you selected; this is a rough outline of how the paragraph or paragraphs concerning this particular subtopic will read. Ask yourself if the order sounds how you would like it to. If so, then move on to the next subtopic you want to present, arranging each pile of note cards as you go. Once you have ordered all of the information for each subtopic, read through all of your note cards in order, starting with the first note card of the first subtopic and finishing with the last note card of the last subtopic. Tweak anything you need to in order to ensure you have the best order for your paper.

Next, write out the main point of each note card in order underneath each relevant subtopic on your outline. It is usually most efficient to organize your outline in the general note-taking format. Bullet subtopics and mark the support details with dashes.

Leave space at the beginning of the outline for ideas for your introduction. Your introduction may or may not use any of your note card information. I often like to choose an interesting and relevant quote or statistic in the introduction in order to catch the reader's attention from the get-go. The first item on your outline, therefore, should include any such information and your thesis. Directly beneath this information, continue on with subtopic #1 and its supporting details. End your outline with a bullet for your conclusion. Your introduction and conclusion will typically include information you brought up in the subtopics of your paper, so you do not need to bother detailing them in too much depth for your outline. As you work, you may think of what you would like to say in these two sections and can add these ideas to your outline at that point.

Writing Style

Some students feel that grading in humanities courses seems to be more subjective than grading in the sciences. This is often because these students have forgotten some of the fundamentals of writing; consequently, they do not always get full credit for their writing's content due to subtle deficiencies in its form. Remember, good academic writing requires appropriate theses, proper paragraph structure, and analysis rather than mere description of the subject matter.

Each paragraph you write should include a distinct topic and concluding sentence. Your paragraph should develop the topic that its topic sentence introduces. The topic sentence should be a paragraph's first sentence unless it follows a transitional sentence that connects it to the prior paragraph. For example, below is a topic sentence for a literary essay.

> *Cormac McCarthy's novel* All the Pretty Horses *is about a sixteen year old boy named John Grady Cole who, in 1948, resolves to leave his family's Texas ranch for Mexico after his maternal grandfather dies, his parents divorce, his girlfriend leaves him for an older boy, and his mother decides to sell the ranch to an oil company.*

The body of the paragraph develops its topic. It explains and provides examples through supporting sentences:

> *The author presents John Grady as decisive; when his best friend Rawlins, who accompanies Grady to Mexico asks him "If I dont* [sic] *go will you go anyways?" Grady responds "I'm already gone" (McCarthy 27). On the way to Mexico a thirteen year old stranger who calls himself Jimmy Blevins, apparently a runaway and a juvenile delinquent, insists on joining them on their trip, against Rawlins' better judgment. Blevins is trouble, and Grady and Rawlins later are blamed for acts that he committed. Some critics believe this to be a coming of age story where Grady starts out as quite immature and naïve in the beginning of the story and, as a result of his trials and tribulations, comes out rather mature by the story's end.*

(Note: *[sic]* is a Latin term meaning *as such*. It is used after the direct quote of erroneous grammar or spelling.) The concluding sentence summarizes the paragraph's main point and may lead into the next paragraph. In this case, since we are considering an introductory paragraph, the concluding sentence is the essay's thesis as well:

However, this essay will demonstrate that Grady suffered not from immaturity and naivety but rather from conflicts of class and culture.

> *You may think it is odd to start writing your paper with the body. After all, you have an outline so shouldn't you know what to say in the introduction? The answer is that writing is a dynamic and fluid process. As you write, you may come up with new ideas or adjust your attitude or angle on the subject. You want your introduction to reflect this. When I began writing this very book you are holding now, I already had an outline over ten pages long. Still, writing the introduction was one of my last steps. I needed to know exactly what I was introducing to you before I could do it right.*

The thesis must make a point that is not self-evident and that *is* based on your insight into the material. You can see that the above is an example of an acceptable thesis because it argues for an insightful interpretation of the subject matter. As you write your essays, remember that summarizing the material is not sufficient to earn a good grade; rather, you must include your personal insights.

The best way to create your paper is by starting with the body, not the introduction. The purpose of an introduction is to introduce your reader to what they are about to read. Considering you have not yet actually written the paper, it will be pretty difficult to accomplish this. Therefore, when you write your paper, you may jot a few sentences and your thesis in the introduction, but expect to add to and improve it later, after writing the body paragraphs.

To write your paper, write the information from your outline and note cards in order using full sentences. It will be best to type your rough draft so that you can neatly edit and change it as you go. Write the entire body of your paper and the concluding paragraph, making sure to address your thesis in the conclusion. The conclusion should be a concentrated summary of your subtopics and a confirmation of your thesis. Once you have completed all of this, read your paper over so that you know what your paper says and concludes. After doing this, you will be able to write an accurate introduction.

Consider all the research you have done and try to use an interesting fact, statistic, or quote to make your opening paragraph catchier. Remember to include your thesis statement at the end of your introduction. Your conclusion should be related to your introductory paragraph and should be supported by the information presented throughout your paper.

When you sit down to write, you want to get something down on paper. Too many students focus on making each sentence they write sound perfect. Do not make this mistake. Successful students know that they have to get the paper actually written before worrying about smaller grammatical and structural details. Keep writing and do not constantly review what you have just written. The purpose of your rough draft is to be a *rough* draft version of your ideas down on paper. After you have completed it you can focus on smoothing it out and editing it.

Also, when you write, don't try to sound like someone other than yourself. Write as you normally would. Avoid using big fancy words for the sake of having big fancy words. You do not need to look in the thesaurus to find longer words than the ones you are using. You want your points to come across clearly and concisely, so it is best to keep your language simple. Avoid awkward sentence structures in an attempt to sound academic and ultra-formal. Stick to proper grammar and correct spelling, and the content of your paper will shine.

If you do want to jazz up your paper with more advanced words than you use in everyday conversation, look for specific vocabulary from classroom discussions. The terms and phrases your teacher used to describe topics similar to yours can be of use to you in your paper. Also, if you repeatedly run across a more advanced term in your research, you may choose to use it. Make sure when you use an advanced word that it fits seamlessly into the diction of your paper. It should read smoothly and be used properly.

Citing Sources

For most research projects, your teacher will expect you to cite your sources. Teachers and school districts make great efforts to prevent students from plagiarizing others' works. As a successful student, you already know that you need to work hard on your own to achieve success and under no circumstances may you plagiarize. Plagiarism is defined as stealing and passing off the ideas or words of another as one's own. You have your own intelligent ideas and thoughts; you don't need to claim anyone else's as your own. When you incorporate information in your paper from somewhere else, cite the source in your work.

In general, your teacher will give you guidelines specifying how you should cite information. Make sure you understand exactly what he or she wants. Students often lose points simply because they did not follow the teacher's instructions concerning how to properly format source citations. Your teacher may require in-text citations and will most definitely want you to include a *bibliography* or *works cited* page listing all of the sources you used in your project. In-text citations are generally accomplished via parenthetical documentation at the end of the sentence containing the cited information. That is, after you include a piece of information from another source, such as a quote, you will immediately and briefly identify the source in parenthesis. This is shown in the writing example given in **Writing Style** on page 161. There are various methods and styles of creating in-text citations; be sure to follow your teacher's guidelines or to ask for further assistance if need be.

Your teacher is the best source to go to in order to find out how he wants you to cite your sources. If for some reason he is unable to offer you adequate direction, check out the guidelines published by the Modern Language Association (MLA). Most high school teachers accept the authority of the MLA for stylistic and research purposes. You can go to your school library and check out an MLA guidebook for more information. There are also many MLA guidelines posted on the internet.

Editing

Once you have completed your rough draft, it is time to refine it. First, you need to edit the paper yourself. To do this, read your paper aloud. Doing so will allow you to recognize any rough transitions or disconnected points. Often, they will just *sound wrong* to you. Furthermore, reading your paper aloud requires you to slow down and give each sentence a thorough review. It is often during this reading that students notice small grammatical and spelling errors.

As you read, make sure your paper fulfills the following criteria:

- Introduction is interesting and accurate
- Introduction includes strong thesis
- Every sentence is clear and makes a point
- Sentences follow in a logical order
- Proper grammar and punctuation are used throughout
- Smooth transitions exist between paragraphs
- Conclusion relates to thesis

Remember, if a sentence does not fulfill the requirements listed above, either delete it or edit it. After you have carefully combed through your paper, you will want to talk to some others to get their feedback as well.

Your parents and peers can offer a fresh perspective and novel insights into your paper. Print out at least one extra copy of your paper and give it to someone who can help you to improve it. Have that individual read your paper and write his or her comments and corrections directly onto the pages. Another option is to send or give an electronic copy of your paper to someone and have that individual add his or her corrections and comments using *Track Changes*.

Pay close attention to the suggestions. Some of the ideas will probably be more important than others. For each one, decide if you think the advice will improve your paper, and revise the relevant sections accordingly. For instance, if someone has difficulty understanding a point you are trying to make, revise that section to correct the problem. Your ideas should be clear from the reader's perspective. Consider what your reader has to say regarding the strongest and weakest parts of your paper, confusing points, and grammatically awkward sections.

If you have another student edit your paper, use caution. Your peers can offer great advice, but you want to be sure no one copies your ideas. If you are working on a topic similar to another student's, do not choose him or her to be an editor for your paper. You worked hard on your paper and do not want your original ideas and efforts copied. Also, your teacher may draw the incorrect conclusion and believe you stole ideas from the other student. As long as you know your ideas will not or cannot be copied by the other student, you can ask him or her to give you feedback on your paper.

Your teacher is the best individual to help you edit your paper. It is better to get quality advice from a few people than to get lots of advice from a bunch of people. Your teacher can give you the quality advice you need. Some students like to bring their paper to other teachers they know to edit their paper. That's great, but each teacher has his or her own preferences. The best feedback you will get on your paper for a class will come from the teacher who will be grading it. If your teacher is willing to give you some pointers on your paper, go for it. If, however, you strongly feel that your paper will get a top grade without advice from your teacher, then go with your intuition; don't feel obligated to ask your teacher for extra help if you don't think you need it.

In addition to your parents, peers, and teachers, your school and local library may offer other editing services. Many schools have free writing centers or English tutors who will help you to edit your paper. Libraries often hold term paper workshops as well and will help you to further develop your writing skills. Actively look for opportunities to improve both your writing skills and your research paper.

Oral Presentations

The research process and overall organization of oral presentations is similar to that discussed above for written assignments. The two differ, of course, in that the oral report must be presented aloud. This means that when you plan your oral report, you will want to avoid words that are difficult to say and complex sentence structures that can strike an audience as awkward or confusing. You will probably also want to create a catchier opening to get people listening. You can appeal to their emotions by telling a personal or relevant story, or you may want to show your own enthusiasm and interest by excitedly telling them a surprising fact or statistic you learned on the subject matter. Another stylistic opener is to use a rhetorical question. Ask the audience a question that will get them thinking about what you have to say.

Typically, before you present your report, you will want to write your speech down on note cards. Note cards are usually better than using sheets of paper because each note card holds only so much information. If you get lost while speaking, it will be easier to find your place on a note card with a few points listed on it rather than on an entire page of written material. Make sure to clearly number your note cards in the order they are to be presented, in case they become disordered at some point.

You can also use other media in your presentation that you are unable to use in a written report. You can draw pictures on the board while speaking, play audio clips, show large pictures or slides using programs such as PowerPoint, or include other visual aids, such as short videos. You may want to give a relevant demonstration, if possible. If you use other sources for information in your presentation, follow your teacher's guidelines concerning how to cite them. He or she may want you to mention them in your talk, include the source titles on your slides, or hand in a paper listing all of your references.

When speaking, it is especially important that you plan your transitions so that they are smooth. I have heard speakers making good points botch their presentations and lose their audiences by failing to connect their points with one another. At times it may be difficult to create a smooth transition between two specific points. If this is the case, you may need to change the order of your presentation, or try introducing the new subject by saying *Next we will consider...* so that your audience is prepared for you to change topics.

Your conclusion should emphasize the main point you want your talk to get across. If you want to persuade your audience to take action for a specific cause, tell them what they can do for the situation and reiterate why they should get involved. If the actions of your audience members would benefit them in some way, be sure to point that out. End your presentation with a final decisive sentence stating your point eloquently and clearly; after hearing your presentation, everyone in your audience should have a good understanding of the topics about which you spoke.

Some students like to say *thank you* at the end of their talk. I have heard speech experts argue both for and against this. You should decide how to end your presentation appropriately by considering your specific speech content and personal speaking style. You want to appear comfortable in front of your class even if you do not feel that way. Having a solid concluding remark can help you in this regard. Plan and memorize what you are going to say at the end of your speech. Keep your eyes on the audience as you speak, and keep your voice steady and strong as you finish up. Many students trail off during their conclusion or begin to walk away from the podium while they are still speaking. It makes them appeared scared. Maybe they are scared or nervous, but the key is not to show it. Stay up there and keep your volume up until you are done saying your last word. Then stand there for one short second and give your audience a brief smile before taking your seat. This will keep you from walking away from your speech before you are finished and will give your audience a good final impression of your presentation.

Many people feel uncomfortable speaking in front of an audience. Let's go over some tips to help you feel more relaxed and at ease while giving the appearance of a professional presentation.

- The key to a good speech is adequate preparation and practice. After writing out your speech, spend time becoming familiar with what you are going to say. Memorize the beginning of your introduction and the end of your conclusion so that you will have a strong start and finish and be able to maintain eye contact at those times. To practice, find an area of space where you can repeatedly speak your presentation out loud.

- Make sure that you know how to operate any media you are including in your presentation and that all such items are clearly visible to your audience. For instance, if you are planning to show your audience a picture, hold it up on one side of a room and have a friend stand on the other side. Determine whether he can see the image from a reasonable distance. If no one else is available, use a mirror and decide for yourself if someone sitting in the back row will be able to see the picture. You may choose to pass the item around the room. If so, plan exactly how and when you will go about doing that.

- Once you feel you have satisfactory familiarity with the content of your presentation, you want to improve your speaking skills and appearance. Practice your talk in front of a mirror so that you can see how you look and improve your eye contact. Do this several times a day every day before your speech is due. When practicing, make sure to hold your note cards down and away from your face. Go through your speech slowly and in a steady clear voice. Do not murmur or allow your voice to shake during your talk. Envision your audience and make eye contact with the imaginary individuals in the audience and with your own eyes in the mirror. There are several other items to check over as well while practicing your speech in front of the mirror:

  o If you have any time requirements, make sure you fulfill them. Many students find that when they give their presentation in class they speak a bit faster than when practicing at home, so take this into consideration as well.

  o Add cues to your note cards to improve your presentation of the subject matter. For instance, while presenting certain information you may want purposely to raise your voice, act excited, or sound suspicious.

  o To improve your overall presentation, there are other cues it would be beneficial to add in as well. Draw periodic smiley faces throughout your note cards to remind yourself to give your audience a confident smile. Draw an eye to remind yourself to look up. During your preparation sessions, practice responding to these cues.

  o When you speak, also make sure you maintain good posture and form. Don't sway nervously or constantly wave your hands around. You can plan to use your hands every so often to emphasize a point, but they should generally remain at your sides or resting on the podium, and your feet should be still and firmly planted on the ground. Also, stand straight with your ears in line with your shoulders; it will make you appear and feel more confident.

  o Do not look down at your note cards out of habit. Only do it when you really need to see what to say next.

• Once you become proficient at the above, it will be helpful to give your talk in front of others. Do it seriously, presenting just as you would in class. An audience of one friend will often bring about the same feelings you get when talking in front of a large group, so it can be helpful to practice for a friend or two to confront any nervousness.

• Wear a professional outfit for your talk that you will feel comfortable wearing in front of your class. This will give you an air of authority and improve the appearance of your presentation. Also, make sure to wear shoes that you can stand in for the duration of your presentation.

- On the day of your speech, try to practice your talk in front of a mirror at least once before going to class. You want to know you have your speech down. Feel confident in yourself and in what you are saying.

- In class, enjoy the other students' presentations, and take deep relaxing breaths in through your nose as you sit and wait for your turn to present. When it is your turn, stand up straight and walk to the podium with good posture. Smile and relax all the muscles in your body, especially your jaw and face. Quiet any fears or self-doubting thoughts running through your mind. You prepared well for this moment, and you are ready to tell your class what you want to present to them. Remember to bring up your note cards and any visual aids you want to show.

- Once you get up to the podium, take a moment to look at your audience, smile, and relax yourself. Then, begin with your memorized introductory lines. Focus on sounding calm and speaking slowly, clearly, and audibly.

- If you have trouble maintaining eye contact with audience members because it makes you nervous, try looking at their foreheads instead. This trick works for many professional speakers, and the audience members can't tell the difference. Slowly turn your head from side to side while you speak so that all sections of your audience feel that you are paying attention to them. It will help your audience to stay involved in what you have to say and can help you to get a better grade.

Follow these tips and you will have a stellar presentation. Feel confident in yourself and in your ability to present well. It is what you say and how you say it that make up the grade your teacher will give you. Before starting your speech, give yourself a positive boost. You know that your speech is great; look forward to sharing it with your classmates and teacher. They are in for a treat!

Summary: Doing Reports

- Choose a research topic for which an abundance of information is available.

- Spend time brainstorming topic ideas from various sources. Your teacher may have good suggestions as well.

- For persuasive pieces for which you do not already have an opinion, declare your position only after doing some preliminary research.

- Print out or photocopy your research material. Then highlight it and note your subtopics in the margins.

- Make note cards that contain the relevant information and label them with the source reference and subtopic category.

- Create a thesis and organize your note cards. Then, create your outline.

- Start your paper by writing the body, then go on to your conclusion, and finish by writing your introduction.

- Let your rough draft have rough edges. You will edit it later.

- Carefully follow your teacher's guidelines concerning how to cite your sources.

- Read your paper aloud to yourself to find areas in need of revision.

- For an oral presentation, memorize your introduction and conclusion and be familiar with the rest of the material. Practice on your own, in front of a mirror, and in front of others.

Parting Message

••

You now possess the skills and character necessary to succeed in school and to prepare yourself for a bright future. Keep focused on the goals and commitments you made. Once you have accomplished these, set new and even more impressive goals. Keep reaching higher as you move up in life.

Remember the principles we focused upon here. Break down anything that is too large to accomplish all at once into well-defined, manageable objectives. Long-term assignments should be broken down into short-term projects, lengthy study periods punctuated by small breaks. Also, keep things simple. There is no use in having unnecessary school supplies or worrying about issues essentially irrelevant to your success. Remain calm and focused, and persevere.

As you progress, review the relevant sections of this book to ensure that you make the best of your academic life. We have gone over every aspect of being a successful student, and you are ready for the challenges that lie ahead. Use the chapter summaries in order to review what you know. Whenever you are faced with a difficult moment, remember all the work you have done and all you know. You have the tools, techniques, and strategies you need in order to succeed.

Stay committed to doing your work and using what you have learned. By doing so, I know you will succeed in your academic endeavors. I invite you to contact me with your thoughts and success stories at <u>SucceedinHighSchool@gmail.com</u>. My best wishes to you in your undertakings both in school and throughout life.

Appendix: Sites for Students

Check out some of the links below to visit websites that can help you in various aspects of your life. Enjoy!

Health:

- http://www.teencentral.net is full of healthful ideas targeted directly towards teenagers; you can also read about your favorite celebrities
- http://www.hungrygirl.com has low calorie recipes for popular food items
- http://teenshealth.org contains information and advice covering many common teen health interests; it also has a special section on study tips

Studying

- http://www.sparknotes.com is a great resource for free study guides in multiple academic disciplines, test preparation lessons, and discussion board interchange
- http://www.cliffnotes.com offers homework help and free literature notes and study guides in many school subjects
- http://www.ratemyprofessor.com is a site at which students from universities and some high schools across the nation post ratings and comments about their professors and teachers
- http://www.ratemyteacher.com allows students in elementary school, middle school, and high school to post ratings and comments about their teachers
- http://www.swapnotes.com is a site at which students post and download notes and old exams from their courses; students also post ratings about their teachers
- http://owl.english.purdue.edu provides instruction regarding English grammar and proper Modern Language Association (MLA) formatting

Fun

- http://www.teenreads.com provides information and features about teens' favorite authors, books, series, and characters
- http://dsc.discovery.com contains games, interesting news items, and cool videos

My Notes

Author's Biography

Grace Charles currently attends medical school at the Mount Sinai School of Medicine in New York City. She enjoys studying medical ethics, writing, teaching, and practicing yoga.

Grace graduated as valedictorian and with a 4.0 GPA from Stern College for Women, Yeshiva University, in New York City. She holds a Bachelor of Arts degree in Biochemistry and an Associate of Arts degree in Judaic Studies. As an undergraduate student, Grace received multiple accolades for her work in biochemistry and organic chemistry, and she conducted novel scientific research that she presented at major scientific conferences around the U.S.

Grace attended Ledyard High School in Connecticut. There she received the Diana Chaney Memorial Award for "her ability to think both creatively and critically, for the maturity and clarity of her writing skills, and for the level of sophistication she has consistently brought to both language and literature assignments." Furthermore, she received the Pfizer Science and Math Scholarship, awarded in recognition of her excellence in those subjects and her aptitude for health-related fields. Moreover, upon her graduation, the Connecticut General Assembly recognized Grace with an official citation as a Ledyard Scholar.

Grace lives in Manhattan with her parents, James and Lorna, and her younger brother Nicholas, a student at the Bronx High School of Science.

6238962R0

Made in the USA
Charleston, SC
30 September 2010